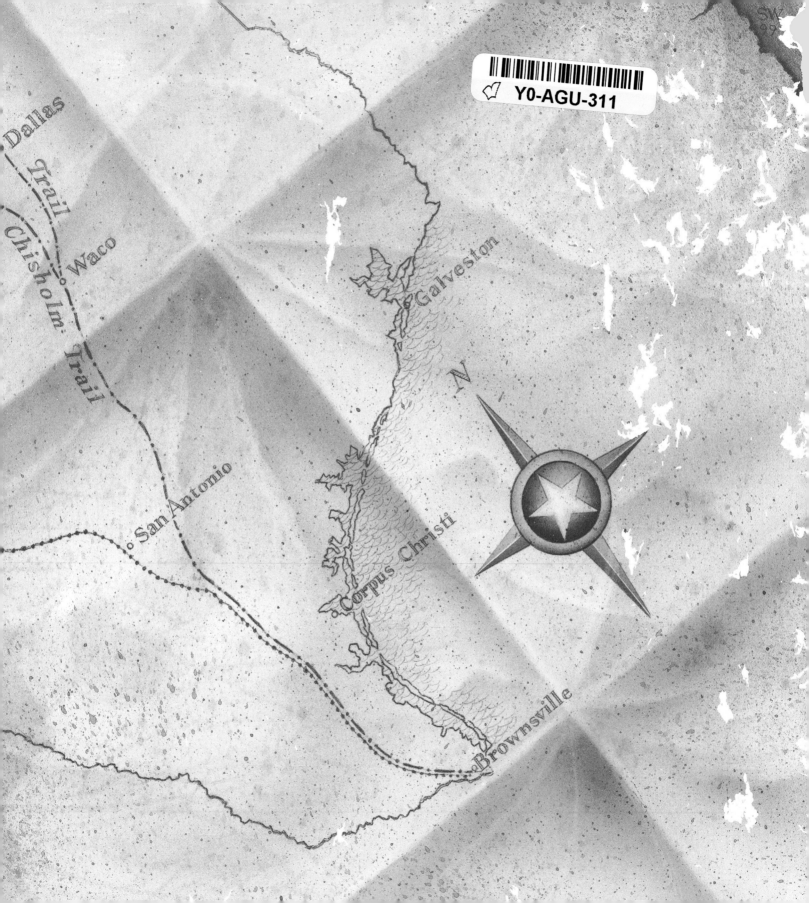

Dallas

Trail

Waco

Chisholm

Trail

San Antonio

Galveston

N

Corpus Christi

Brownsville

TEXAS COWBOY COOKING

TEXAS COWBOY COOKING

TOM PERINI

WITH PASCHAL FOWLKES

FOREWORD BY ROBERT DUVALL

TIME
LIFE
BOOKS

ALEXANDRIA, VIRGINIA

TIME® LIFE BOOKS

Time-Life Books is a division of Time Life Inc.

TIME LIFE INC.
President and CEO: Jim Nelson

TIME-LIFE TRADE PUBLISHING
Vice President and Publisher: Neil Levin
Senior Director of Acquisitions
and Editorial Resources: Jennifer Pearce
Director of New Product Development: Carolyn Clark
Director of Marketing: Inger Forland
Director of New Product Development: Teresa Graham
Director of Trade Sales: Dana Hobson
Director of Custom Publishing: John Lalor
Director of Special Markets: Robert Lombardi
Director of Design: Kate L. McConnell

TEXAS COWBOY COOKING
Project Manager: Jennie Halfant
Technical Specialist: Monika Lynde
Production Manager: Carolyn Bounds
Quality Assurance: Jim King, Stacy L. Eddy

Printed in U.S.A.

Pre-Press Services, Time-Life Imaging Center

10 9 8 7 6 5 4 3 2 1

TIME-LIFE is a trademark of Time Warner Inc., and
affiliated companies.

Library of Congress Cataloging-in-Publication Data

Perini, Tom, 1943-
   Texas cowboy cooking / Tom Perini.
     p. cm.
   ISBN 0-7370-2037-7
   1. Cookery, American--Southwestern style.
 2. Cookery--Texas. I. Title.

   TX715.2.S69 P47 2000
   641.59764--dc21   99-089478

Books produced by Time-Life Trade Publishing are available at a special bulk discount for promotional and premium use. Custom adaptations can also be created to meet
your specific marketing goals. Call 1-800-323-5255.

A Judd Publishing Book
Book Design by Caroline Brock
Food Photography by Mark Davis
Ranching Photography by Bob Moorhouse
Maps and Illustrations by Stephen R. Wagner
Research by Katie Dickie Stavinoha

*To the Perini Family—
especially to my mother, Maxine,
and my late father, V.C. "Bud,"
who have always encouraged me
to follow my dreams.*

FOREWORD

I got my first taste of Tom Perini's cooking a few years back when I was working on a movie called *Stars Fell on Henrietta*. We were fortunate to be filming near Buffalo Gap, Texas—home of the Perini Ranch Restaurant—and after Clint Eastwood and I ate our first meal there, the cast and crew returned for dinner as often as we could. I've always loved traveling and I've eaten all over the world, and let me tell you, there's nothing like stumbling upon really great local food.

It's hard to say what my favorite Perini dish is; in fact, I'll order everything from the steaks to the bread pudding. There's no pretense to Tom's food, just a lot of flavor. I wish I'd had Tom along when I was filming *Lonesome Dove,* because his is the kind of food my character Augustus McCrae ate on the cattle drive—wholesome, authentic, delicious food that can be cooked in one pot or over an open fire. It's best enjoyed sitting around the chuck wagon, and it just tastes like the American West. If you're looking for true cowboy cooking without compromise, Perini Ranch Steakhouse is the place to go.

I haven't yet made my way back to Buffalo Gap, but the area, the people, and the food are really the Texas experience that I'd like to return to. Fortunately, Tom can sometimes be coaxed into driving his wagon back East—and even stopping by with his cowboys to cook for me and my friends right here in my backyard. Now with Tom Perini's new cookbook, *Texas Cowboy Cooking,* we can create his delicious meals at home, even when he and his chuckwagon are back in Buffalo Gap!

Good food is one of my passions and now that I have my own restaurant, The Rail Stop, here in my hometown of The Plains, Virginia, I can appreciate what it takes to create unique recipes and serve excellent food. My friend Tom Perini is one of the best at what he does—authentic cowboy cooking. Now that he's sharing his secrets with us in this cookbook, I might even ask my chef to borrow a recipe or two for The Rail Stop. As far as I'm concerned, you can't go wrong with cooking advice from Tom—he knows his biscuits and beans as well as he knows his beef.

Robert Duvall

CONTENTS

INTRODUCTION 8

The birth of a legend: Here's a little background on what—and who—shaped this part of the country, and how and why I came to be a cowboy cook.

BEVERAGES AND STARTERS 20

Cowboys work hard, play hard, and have been known to drink hard. Here are a few mild-mannered cocktails and full-flavored appetizers.

BEEF AND OTHER MAIN DISHES 68

This is obviously the backbone of my cooking, and here are all sorts of ways to do it. I've even thrown in a few alternatives because not everybody eats beef with every meal—even in Texas.

SOUPS, STEWS AND BREADS 110

From hardy grazing pots to delicate flavors to the infamous Son of a Gun, these are meals in themselves—plus plenty of options for things to sop them up.

SIDE DISHES 144

These are my sleepers. They're great with any main course, and many even stand up on their own.

DESSERTS 164

Even rough-and-tumble cowpokes have a soft spot for sweets, and here are a few treats that are probably a little more appealing than sweetbreads.

INDEX   188
ACKNOWLEDGMENTS   191

INTRODUCTION

INTRODUCTION: COOKING FOR THE COWBOYS

My heroes have always been cowboys—real cowboys. I'm not talking about Roy Rogers or John Wayne twirling six-guns and chasing stage robbers. I didn't grow up with the Hollywood images that kids elsewhere looked up to; I had the real thing. The well-groomed western stars don't hold a candle to my role models: the hard-working, hard-playing characters, with whose sweat the state of Texas was tamed. And it's no accident that Hollywood cowboys are such cool customers; they're polished-up versions of the men who wore dusty boots, hats and chaps, and had that twinkle in their eyes that said, "Give me a job and I'll get it done." They get up early in the morning, they work in extreme conditions without complaint and they're always hungry. Maybe that's why I love to cook for them. Surprisingly, these romantic notions of cowboy life have actually held true in my experience as rancher, cook and restaurateur.

The Cowboy, detail; Frederic Remington; oil on canvas; ca. 1902; courtesy Amon Carter Museum, Fort Worth, Texas.

It was the Texas Longhorn that really made the cowboy famous. Long before the latter left their bootprints in Texas dirt, wild cattle roamed what was then a sea of grass. Texas cattle came from Mexico, and

11

The Bucker; *Charles M. Russell; pencil, watercolor and gouache on paper; 1904; courtesy Sid Richardson Collection of Western Art, Fort Worth, Texas.*

most Mexican cattle came from Spain. Columbus brought the first Spanish cattle to Santo Domingo (now Haiti and the Dominican Republic), and by 1521, treasure hunters like Don Hernando Cortés had brought them to the mainland. Breeds like the old Spanish Corriente freely multiplied, and many wandered northward. So, 200 years later, when European explorers ventured into South Texas, they found a hardy breed of cattle living comfortably. They had long, pointed horns nature made to protect young'ns and turf, but subsequent settlers along the Rio Grande recognized these animals as a means to potentially prosper.

The earliest Texas rancheros let their cattle wander where the grass and water took them until the springtime "cow hunts"—what then passed for roundups. Cattle production was a whim of nature; no rancher could predict the paternity of his cattle's offspring. The Anglo-Celtic settlers in the early 1800s were accustomed to penning their animals. In Texas, however, there were no fences, and on the open ranges many of the docile English-based breeds were promptly whipped into submission by the tough Longhorn prairie cattle.

FEEDING A NATION

Today's ranching is rooted in the days between Texas's independence in 1836 and the Civil War, when various groups were given land to settle. As early as 1832, Anglo cattlemen were trailing steers to markets in New Orleans, but in the 1860s people really started to see the potential of the cattle business. A lot of men came home from the Civil War with nothing and moved west to opportunity—often to Texas. The North was thriving and had developed an appetite for beef. So now the question was how to transport huge herds thousands of miles. Enterprising cattlemen began rounding up cattle and driving them north toward the northern and eastern markets. Some herds were driven straight to Chicago, and I've even heard of one being taken all the way to New York City. This, of course, didn't last long, as the herds would trample fences, crops and just about anything else in their way. It was right around this time that a man named Joseph McCoy extended the railroad west of Kansas City to a little town called Abilene, Kansas. The railhead became a meeting point for Texas ranchers and East Coast buyers.

13

Bucking Bronco; rodeo event, Texas Cowboy Reunion, Stamford, Texas; photographer unknown; courtesy Swenson Land and Cattle Company archives.

To reach the railroads, cattle drives traversed pretty rough country. Young men left home at an early age to cowboy on the great cattle drives. There were probably 35,000 men who saddled up for these several-month trips, but it wasn't for everyone. Albany, Texas, rancher and historian Bob Green tells of a Texas youth who

The romance of the West appealed to folks as soon as word traveled east. By the early 1900s, books and magazines regularly treated readers to stories of Western life. Among the few who trekked west for an eyeful were Frederic Remington (1861–1909) and Charles M. Russell (1865–1926), who became pillars in the Western art movement.

Remington excelled in depicting the Western frontier in his illustrations in *Harper's Weekly* and other magazines, and later through his bronze sculpture. Remington's work brought the fantasy out of the mundane efforts of those inhabiting the West, while illuminating the relationship of the cowboys to the land. Russell, on the other hand, is seen as providing a reality-based observation of that same body. His paintings captured a vivid picture of his life until 1893—though it was not until 1911 that he became well known for his artistry. The efforts of both men captured the rustic, romantic notion of the American West.

Photographs also played an important role in whetting America's appetite for Western culture, well into the 20th century. Dorothea Lange (1895–1965) effectively chronicled the plight of the American farmer during and after the Great Depression. Erwin E. Smith (1881–1947), a Texas cowboy-turned-photographer/sculptor, also left his mark on the images of ranching life. His photos honestly captured the daily workings of Texas ranch life.

signed on to drive a herd to the northern plains. After a few months on the job, his boss noticed him riding his horse against the herd of cattle and asked him what he was doing. The young cowboy replied, "I'm going to get my coat." The boss asked him where might his coat be and the cowboy replied, "Texas."

During almost three decades of cattle driving, 6 to 10 million head of cattle walked the trails to the railroads. There was fierce competition to lure the cattle drives: Every town wanted the drovers spending money in their saloons, but it was Fort Worth's success in hosting the Chisholm Trail—and 51,000 live cattle by 1877—that earned its claim to "Cowtown."

Just as communities tried to attract the trail drives and buffalo trade, so they competed for the railroad. Places like Buffalo Gap boomed in those early days, but when the railroads passed them over, their demise was imminent. The expansion of the railroad, especially to Fort Worth, was the beginning of the end of the long trail drives. And the invention and widespread use of barbed wire brought on the beginnings of the modern Texas rancher. With fencing, ranchers had some control over their operations. They could import a Shorthorn that they remembered from their homeland and be sure that he could lay his mark on a crop of offspring. The cows, for the most part, were still of the original Texas breeding, but generation by generation, Texas cattle were changing.

ON THE WAGON

Cattle ranching and trail driving was for one purpose: supplying the demand for beef. But cowboys did not sit down for a big steak dinner every night. When *vaqueros* (the origin of the English word, "buckaroo"), or cowboys, were beating the Texas brush on cow hunts, they packed several days' worth of jerky, hardtack and maybe a little coffee. And since these guys were pretty scattered, feeding them wasn't a cow boss's main concern. But on the drives and at roundup, and later, on the far reaches of the ranches, you had a bunch of cowboys to feed without the convenience of a

15

The Virginian; Charles M. Russell; pen and ink drawing on paper; ca. 1911; courtesy Amon Carter Museum, Fort Worth, Texas.

kitchen. This problem was solved by Charles Goodnight, famous trail driver and Texas cattleman, who is credited with the introduction of what became the nerve center of trail life —the chuck wagon.

Pretty soon, ranches were using chuck wagons and their cooks right there on the property. Wagons would set up at the roundup. Again, the fare wasn't fancy, but it was tasty and filling. When cowboys weren't involved in roundup, meals were served at the cookshack. This was a separate building, set slightly away from barns and houses because of the threat of fire. Cowboys would have breakfast in the morning, ride in for lunch if they were close enough, and have supper before hitting the bunkhouse.

Cowboy Camp
During the Roundup;
Charles M. Russell;
oil on canvas; ca. 1887;
courtesy Amon Carter
Museum, Fort Worth, Texas.

Long the center of a ranch, the cookshack is also very much in use today. Because of technology, roundups and "cow work" may take fewer cowboys, but those working will gather at the cookshack to eat, report in and receive orders for the day. The cookshack is also used by the ranch family as the same kind of meeting place and social gathering point. Whether they're celebrating a wedding, a birth or a successful roundup, ranchers love to entertain. And it's considered bad manners to turn down the offer of a meal, whether it be in the shade of a mesquite tree, on a pickup's tailgate or at the cookshack. On the Perini Ranch, the steakhouse is now where people gather, but the original cookshack holds a lot of memories and is still one of my favorite spots.

NATIVE SON

I'm a Texan, born and bred, but a long way from those frontier settlers. When I started the Perini Cattle Co. here in Buffalo Gap, we used an old chuck wagon, and I liked hanging around the wagon and really enjoyed cooking. Some of the big ranches around knew this, and they started asking me to help with some of their parties. In the early '70s we took chuck wagons all over, and I learned from guys who'd been doing it forever. It was around this time that my late friend and ranching mentor Watt Matthews sat me down. "You know, Tom," he said, "if you really like the cooking, you ought to get serious about it. You can do

more for the industry cooking beef than raising it." He was a very close friend of my father's, and ever since I was a little boy, I was going over to the Matthews Ranch. After my father died, Watt was sort of a father figure to me. So I started the catering business in earnest. Before long, we were cooking for the Texas Cowboy Reunion in Stamford, the largest amateur rodeo in the state.

Then in 1983, I decided to open the restaurant on the ranch. It was just an old barn that we converted to a roadhouse with minimal food service. There was no sign on the highway, but word got out. It's a true destination restaurant: a Texas version of building a baseball diamond in the middle of a cornfield. When you live in a town with 499 people and you have a steakhouse out in the middle of a ranch, they have to come to you. They aren't just driving by. Our food is a spin-off of the old chuck-wagon and ranch food, and the restaurant is set up like a ranch cookshack. From the outside, you'd never know it was a restaurant. I used to have people drive up and come in and say they were looking for this steakhouse out in the country.

We've got the restaurant open five nights a week, we're busy catering year round and I've even got myself involved in the mail-order business with a mesquite-smoked pepper tenderloin— but that's another story. Over the years, I've cooked in a lot of places: from the James Beard House in New York to vineyards in

A New Year on
the Cimarron;
Frederic Remington;
oil on canvas; 1901;
courtesy Museum of
Fine Arts, Houston,
Texas; The Hogg
Brothers Collection;
gift of Miss Ima Hogg.

19

California, from Mexico to the Texas Governor's Mansion. I
even brought the chuck wagon and 5,000 pounds of mesquite
on a cooking tour of Japan. But I still love to roll out the
chuck wagon right here on the ranch.

The recipes we've chosen for this book reflect the simple
pleasures of Texas cowboy and ranch life. They're not fancy, they're
just good home cooking: real chuck. I want to reawaken your taste
buds and stir your memories. We pass recipes and cooking tech-
niques from one generation to the next, from a period of history
rich in tradition. I like to promote this tradition, whether you're in
Texas, California, North Dakota or New York City.

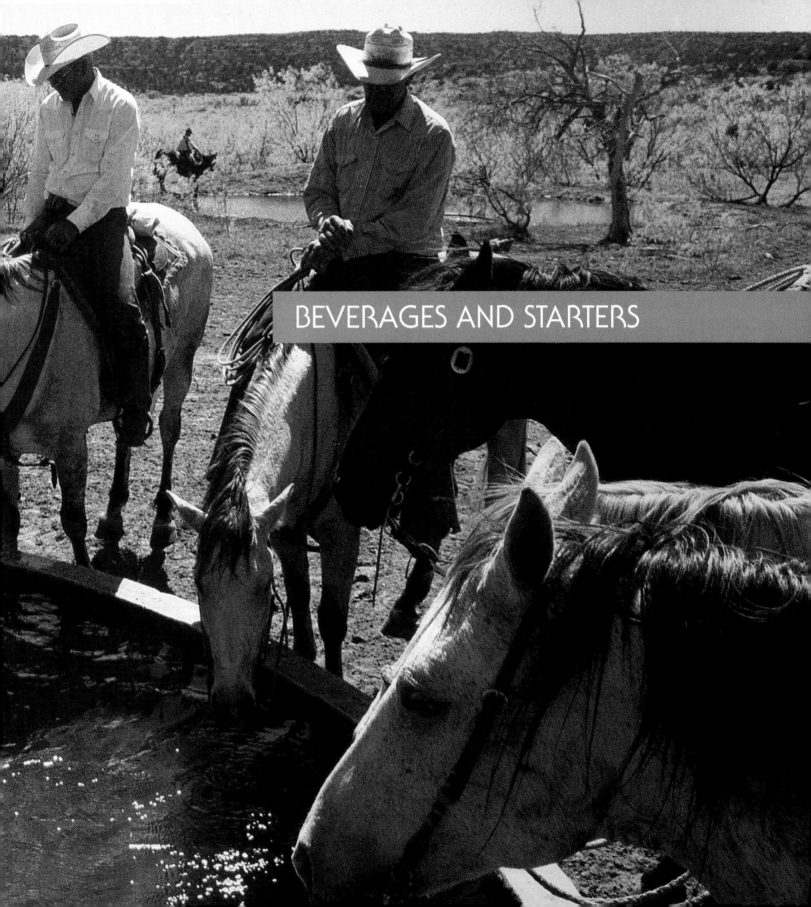

BEVERAGES AND STARTERS

BEVERAGES AND STARTERS

There comes a time everyday, somewhere between the end of the workday and dinnertime, when Texans—like most people everywhere else, I imagine—sit down for some refreshment. If you ever found yourself at the headquarters of Lambshead Ranch around five o'clock, you'd hear my late friend Watt Matthews say, "Of course you'll stay and have a tod," and you did. This was short for toddy and it's a Texas tradition.

Texas cowboys like their bourbon and it's often ordered with a splash of water, known as bourbon and branch, as in branch water. Another cowboy favorite is a bloody beer—which is just beer and tomato juice—but I suspect the juice is just another excuse for a drink in the morning. It is rumored to be a pretty good hangover cure. Cowboys work hard, play hard, and have been known to drink hard, but we certainly don't limit ourselves to the rough-and-tumble. The drinks in this chapter are variations on classic cocktails and picnic punches, but they are all personal favorites, all typical Texas and all damn good.

Counterclockwise from left: Ranch House Lemon Cooler (page 30), Mesquite-a-Rita (page 27), The Martinez (page 29) and a Bucket of Beer (page 37).

23

Incidentally, when I say jigger I mean about an ounce and a quarter to an ounce and a half, but, like everything else here, if you like it a little stronger use a little more, and, of course, vice versa.

APPETIZERS: STARTING OUT

Now there aren't too many chuck-wagon cooks walking around with a silver tray of canapés, back then or today, but there are a lot of dishes that come right out of the cow camps with which we can do exactly that. And I love to really blow people away with a great hors d'oeuvre before they even sit down. At the restaurant, the pre-meal favorite is generally a smaller version of a main course, ribs—but I like to mix it up a little. Here are some starters that range from variations on old Mexican standards to a bite-sized taste of Texas.

Whether you're looking for a snack for two before dinner, have 20 people in the backyard, or even expect 60 for dinner, I think we've got a pretty wide selection of hors d'oeuvres. While many of them are what I call one-bite snacks, they can be paired with a small salad to make a nice light meal. As always, I encourage you to use them to fit your needs.

SALADS: BEANS AND GREENS

Now I realize that salad doesn't exactly jump to mind when you think about chuck-wagon fare, but it is served in cookshacks, in all forms, all over the state. Plus, not to take advantage of all this great produce we have down here would be just a shame.

These salads are traditional Texas dishes. If you're entertaining in the summertime, you can't have things that are too delicate. Whether it's on the back of a wagon or in a cow camp or in your backyard, a lot of things are done outside. So most of the salads that we use are geared for that; the Texas Caviar (page 57) and the Black Bean and Roasted Corn Salad (page 56) are good hardy additions to any meal. A bean salad is just not going to wilt.

PERINI MARTINI

It's got a nice ring to it, doesn't it? This is a real shaken martini; just shake the hell out of it—until it gets so cold you can't hold the shaker. It's actually a dirty martini (in that we use the olive brine), and we add our own Texas touch of olives stuffed with jalapeños. I also like using the Tito's (the only vodka made in Texas) because it has a distinct taste that complements the kick of the pepper. It's a good special-occasion drink; it's real cold and real strong, but it's for the serious drinker. Know when to say when, or this one can get you in trouble.

2 jiggers Tito's Texas Vodka
   (or vodka of your choice, even gin)
1 teaspoon dry vermouth
1 teaspoon brine from the olives
1 large green olive, stuffed with jalapeño

Fill a large martini glass with ice cubes and a little water and let chill. In a shaker, combine the vodka, vermouth, brine and a scoop of ice, and shake vigorously. Empty the glass, and strain vodka mixture over the jalapeño-stuffed olive. *Makes 1 drink.*

MESQUITE-A-RITA

This is a recipe developed and served at the steakhouse. It's a top-of-the-line margarita, and it's strong; it's not a fru-fru drink. It's done the way the Mexicans do it: using good tequila and fresh lime juice. I have a big mesquite stump out back and someday I'd like to hollow it out and sink a jug of Mesquite-a-Rita in there with a tap on it—like maple syrup in Vermont. I might just make up a story about how the Indians and the buffalo hunters used to hang around here because of this amazing tree. We served these Mesquite-a-Ritas on our most recent trip to the James Beard House for a Cowboy Christmas in New York City. About 15 minutes into the party, the bartenders were calling for more Mesquite-a-Ritas, and we knew the New Yorkers were having a Texas-style good time! Our evening was a success and the guests loved their first Cowboy Christmas—the jury is still out whether it was the food or the cocktails.

1 jigger Cuervo Gold Tequila
½ jigger Grand Marnier
1 jigger Triple Sec
1 jigger freshly squeezed lime juice
Lime slices, to serve

Rub rim of an old-fashioned glass with a fresh lime, quartered. Dip rim in coarsely ground salt. Combine ingredients in shaker, shake well and pour over ice. Garnish with a lime wheel. *Makes 1 drink.*

COWBOY BLOODY MARY

So called because a cowboy is never far from his horseradish. The Bloody Mary is a standard drink, but we do something a little different—we use horseradish and we garnish with a pickled okra. This gives it kind of a unique flavor. It makes a pretty drink and the horseradish gives it an extra bite. Then there's the variation on this that I like to call the "Bloody Shame." It's a virgin and a delicious drink, but it's a bloody shame there's no vodka in it.

1 jigger vodka
5 ounces tomato juice
1/2 teaspoon prepared horseradish
1 1/2 teaspoons Worcestershire sauce
Salt, pepper and celery salt, to taste
3–4 dashes of Tabasco
1 fresh blanched or pickled okra (page 48)

Moisten rim of glass and coat in celery salt. Combine the vodka, tomato juice and horseradish and mix well. Pour over ice. Add the Worcestershire sauce, salt, pepper and celery salt, to taste. Add Tabasco, to taste. Garnish with okra. *Makes 1 drink.*

Works well to make by the pitcher.

2-quart pitcher
1 1/2 cups vodka
48 ounces tomato juice
3 tablespoons horseradish
1/2 cup Worcestershire sauce
Salt, pepper and celery salt, to taste
2 teaspoons Tabasco
10–12 pickled okra

THE MARTINEZ

This is a two-stage drink invented by my older brother, Vee, who takes great delight in this honor. This drink goes well with good conversation in the backyard or at the kitchen counter before dinner. Obviously, this is another one that really packs a punch, both from the tequila and the pepper, and it's always a good conversation starter. Vee says that your lips should actually tingle a little if it's made properly, and I think they probably tingle a lot if it's not. It definitely has a bite.

2 jiggers Cuervo Gold Tequila
Splash of Triple Sec
1–2 teaspoons brine from pickled jalapeño, to taste
¼ fresh lime
Whole pickled jalapeño
1 bottle Mexican beer, your favorite

Fill a large martini glass with ice cubes and a little water and let chill. In a shaker, combine the tequila, Triple Sec and jalapeño brine, and shake vigorously with ice. Then empty the glass, rub the rim with the lime, dip in salt. Then strain the mixture over whole jalapeño in glass. Drink some of the Martinez then start adding your favorite beer. Repeat until both are empty. (You may also try a Martinez en Los Rocos, in a Collins glass filled with ice.) *Makes 1 drink.*

29

Cowboy siesta; *photographer unknown; courtesy Texas and Southwestern Cattle Raisers Foundation, Fort Worth, Texas.*

BOURBON MILK PUNCH

I think of this as a standard Sunday morning brunch drink. We Texans drink a lot of bourbon, and though this is an early-in-the-day drink, two ounces is a pretty good shot of bourbon—but this is a socially acceptable way to do it. It's right up there with Bloody Marys and Mimosas when we cater a brunch.

2 ounces bourbon
1 cup whole milk
1 teaspoon powdered sugar
Freshly grated nutmeg

Combine the bourbon, milk and sugar, shake with ice, and strain into a Collins glass. Sprinkle with freshly grated nutmeg. *Makes 1 drink.*

RANCH HOUSE LEMON COOLER

This is a refreshing summer toddy, whose contrasting salt/tart flavors are so good at cutting the heat of the sun and the bite of the liquor.

1 jigger vodka
½ lemon
Club soda

Salt the rim of an old-fashioned glass. Pour vodka over ice, squeeze the lemon into the vodka and fill the glass with club soda. *Makes 1 drink.*

HOT TODDY

A great cure for a cold . . . or the winter chill of a Texas "blue norther."

1 jigger bourbon
Juice of 1 lemon
Lemon peel strip
2 tablespoons honey
¼ cup hot water
Cinnamon stick
2–3 whole cloves

Combine all the ingredients in a microwaveable cup. Heat until steaming. Taste to check sweetness. Add a little more honey, if needed. *Makes 1 drink.*

TEQUILA SHOT

Now a real cowboy wouldn't have a tequila shot served up in a salted martini glass. He would be a lot less dainty and use this technique.

1 jigger premium tequila
Dash of salt
Lime wedge

Pour the tequila into a shot glass. Make fist with your left hand, lick the spot between your thumb and finger and cover the spot with salt. Lick the salt from your hand, shoot the tequila and then bite the wedge of lime. You'll feel like a cowboy. *Makes 1 drink.*

SUMMER SANGRIA

This is a very refreshing drink, and with a lot of peaches, it's a real Texas treat. It's great to sit out in the backyard with when you have some people over and it's easy to make in big batches. One of the nice things about the Summer Sangria is that you can throw in any of the fresh fruits that happen to be in season. We've used berries, honeydew melon, cantaloupe, even figs.

1 liter white wine
1 lemon or lime, thinly sliced
3–4 tablespoons sugar OR honey
1 peach, fresh and ripe, sliced into thin wedges
1 seedless orange, thinly sliced
4–5 sprigs fresh mint

Mix the wine and lemon slices with sugar or honey, and stir until dissolved. Add the peach, orange slices and mint. *Makes 1½ quarts.*

33

COWBOY COFFEE

This recipe was given to me by my late friend and famous chuck-wagon cook Richard Bolt. Richard used it thousands of times in his days at the Pitchfork Ranch, the 6666 Ranch and a host of other ranches and camps. Though I've given it a twist of my own, this is a real cowboy recipe. Most often the coffee was the legendary Arbuckles coffee, which came in 1-pound sacks and 50-pound boxes. In the 1870s, John Arbuckle put a stick of peppermint in each bag. He considered it a "premium" but chuck-wagon cooks used it as incentive to get cowboys to grind the next day's supply of coffee beans.

Water
Coffee

The night before, fill your one gallon coffeepot with room-temperature water to about an inch below the spout. Then pour in 1 to 1½ cups of coffee grounds (depending on how strong you like your coffee) and let it sit overnight. In the morning put it over a low fire and bring it to a simmer. Then take it off the flame, pour out a little to clean the spout and dash the pot with cold water (this makes the grounds sink to the bottom). *Makes 16 cups.*

HOT CHOCOLATE

Great on a cold night.

1 heaping tablespoon
    unsweetened cocoa
1 tablespoon sugar
Pinch of ground cinnamon

Pinch of ground cloves
2 tablespoons water
1 cup milk

In a large mug, mix the cocoa, sugar, cinnamon, clove, and water together until smooth. Add the milk and heat in the microwave or in a small saucepan. Top with whipped cream, if you like. *Serves 1.*

RED SANGRIA

This is a favorite south-of-the-border drink because it's easily doubled or tripled and looks great in big glass pitchers. You might serve this with Mexican food or just as a fun way to drink wine.

35

2 oranges
1 lemon
1 lime
½ cup sugar
Fifth of burgundy (750 mL)
8–10 ounces club soda
Ice

A ranch chuck wagon being brought to the Stamford, Texas, Cowboy Reunion; photographer unknown; ca. 1930; courtesy Swenson Land and Cattle Company archives.

Cut one of the oranges, the lemon and the lime into quarters. Squeeze the juices from the fruits into a pitcher and add the rinds and sugar. Stir with a wooden spoon. Add wine and soda and mix well. Pour into tall, ice-filled glasses. Garnish each glass with a slice from the second orange. *Serves 6.*

WINES OF TEXAS

Oil and cattle are one thing, but wine in Texas? You bet your boots. There are a number of Texas wineries that are making some very good wine, both red and white. In fact, our menu at the steakhouse offers almost exclusively Texas wines; the only exception is a wine made in California by Fess Parker, who grew up nearby in San Angelo, Texas. His favorite family recipe, Parker Burgers, is on page 87.

Like our cattle, Texas wine owes much to the Spanish explorers, who brought vine cuttings to plant in this uncharted territory. In 1659 they set them down in the first Spanish settlement and began cultivating grapevines for sacramental wine. But grapes were not foreign to Texas: Mustang grapes were being used by winemaking settlers by the mid-1800s. Texas's first winery, Val Verde Winery in Del Rio on the Rio Grande, was established in 1883. By 1900, there were 26 wineries in the state, but only Val Verde survived Prohibition.

In the early 1970s, winemakers rediscovered Texas's potential. The sandy, well-drained soils; warm, sunny days; cool nights; low humidity and constant air movement are similar to some of the great French wine regions. Today, there are 25 wineries operating in the Lone Star State, making it ninth in the country in wine production.

TEXAS TEA

Here is a great alcohol-free way to cool off in the summertime.

1 cup sugar
1 teaspoon salt
1 cup hot water
1 quart tea, freshly brewed and cooled
Juice of 4 lemons (½ cup)
2 cups orange juice
4–5 sprigs fresh mint
Slices of lemon, lime and orange

Mix the sugar, salt and hot water until completely dissolved. Add the tea, lemon and orange juices and mint, and serve over lots of ice with additional slices of lemon, lime and orange. *Serves 6 to 8.*

OLD-FASHIONED EGGNOG

This is a favorite Christmas tradition with the Perini family. The eggnog is served with desserts following Christmas dinner and is a very elegant way to end the meal. Of course, it can also accompany hors d'oeuvres.

6 large eggs, separated, at room temperature
¾ cup sugar
2 cups milk
½ cup bourbon
½ cup brandy
2 cups heavy whipping cream, chilled
Freshly grated nutmeg

In a large bowl, beat the egg whites (using an electric mixer) just until soft peaks form. Gradually beat in half (6 tablespoons) of the sugar until stiff peaks form. Set aside.

In another bowl, beat the egg yolks (using an electric mixer) and add the remaining 6 tablespoons of sugar. Beat until the mixture is light in color—about 2 minutes. Beat in the milk, bourbon and brandy. Add the whites and gently fold to barely mix together.

In a chilled large bowl, beat the heavy cream until stiff. Add to the egg mixture and fold in until the eggnog is smooth. Cover and chill at least 4 hours or overnight.

37

Pour the eggnog into a large punch bowl and sprinkle the grated nutmeg on top. Serve chilled. *Serves 12 to 15.*

BUCKETS OF BEER

Here at the steakhouse, when you order a bucket of beer, your waitress brings you an iced pail containing seven beers (you select the brand or assortment of brands) and you pay for only six beers. This way you always have an ice-cold beer ready and waiting.

38

CALF FRIES

This is a real rancher's hors d'oeuvre, probably anywhere in the country, and it's delicious. The only problem you have with calf fries is trying to explain to someone what they are. If you're in the cattle business, you're very familiar with this. In the spring and the fall, when ranchers have a roundup or work the young calves, they "cut" the bull calves so that they grow bigger. The cowboys spare the biggest and strongest bulls for future use and the rest provide calf fries. They make dudes a little nervous, but they really are very good, and they don't taste anything like chicken. We did these at the James Beard House in New York and it was a very ticklish situation. A lot of people loved them until they found out what they'd been eating; you could just see the color in their faces change. But they're a real delicacy; I mean, you save them for your special occasions. Sometimes the real cowboys will castrate the calves, put a shovel over a fire pit and cook the calf fries right there. I'm not that tough.

Calf fries	Oregano
Flour	Parsley
Salt	Garlic salt
Black pepper	Paprika
Crushed red pepper	

Remove the outside membrane and wash each calf fry thoroughly. The average calf fry is about the size of a hen or goose egg. Then slice it in half and peel back the second thin covering. The calf fry can now be quartered into bite-sized pieces and rolled in a mixture of flour, salt, pepper and spices. Fry in a skillet with hot grease until golden brown. *Allow several pieces per person.*

Hint: If the calf fries are frozen, they are easier to peel and handle while cleaning.

BACON-WRAPPED DOVE BREAST

Hunting is extremely popular in Texas, and Labor Day dove hunting is a regular Texas tradition. This is a very common way to serve your smaller game, as appetizers or hors d'oeuvres. It's something that can easily be passed around at cocktail hour, and it's got a lot of good flavors. When you cook the jalapeños, you take out a lot of the fire. I mean, they'll still get your attention when you bite into them, but you won't drop to your knees.

6 dove breast halves*
2 slices uncooked bacon
2 fresh jalapeños (depending on their size),
   seeded and cut into 6 thin strips

Preheat oven to 350°. Split and bone dove breast. Cut each strip of bacon into 3 pieces. Fold dove breast around jalapeño strip and wrap in piece of bacon. Secure with toothpick. Bake for about 50 minutes, or until bacon is done. This can also be prepared on the grill. Follow same preparation instructions and cook over the fire. *Serves 6.*

*Quail breasts or boneless, skinless chicken thighs may be substituted.

39

PICO DE GALLO

Pico de gallo is an uncooked salsa that should be made with the freshest ingredients. Use good fresh vegetables and chop your onions and tomatoes into pretty good-sized chunks; that way it'll really stay on your chips when you dip them. Make a big bowl of this and keep it in a crock in the refrigerator, and it'll stay fresh for two or three days. Then you can put a scoop on your scrambled eggs or put it on top of your nachos or anything else. Remember, always rinse fresh vegetables thoroughly before preparation. It's also a good idea to let some of the tomato juice run off before adding them; this keeps the "Pico" from being too liquid.

2–3 fresh ripe tomatoes, diced
½ large white onion, diced
3 fresh medium jalapeños, seeded and diced
1 tablespoon freshly chopped cilantro
Salt, to taste

Combine all the ingredients. *Makes 2 cups.*

GUACAMOLE

This is, of course, from Mexico and, like the "Pico", you can put it on practically anything. It's served a lot in Texas partly because it can be a really refreshing taste, particularly when it's hot out. But remember not to overmix it; I like to maintain the texture of the fresh avocado, so I don't want it too creamy. I also like to serve a bowl of guacamole with a spoonful of pico de gallo on top. And a good trick, if you're making it a little beforehand, is to leave the pits in the bowl until just before you serve it—this keeps the guacamole from getting brown too quickly.

3 medium ripe avocados, halved, pitted and peeled
¼ cup finely chopped white onion
1 tomato, small and ripe, finely chopped
2 tablespoons fresh lime juice
1 fresh jalapeño, seeded and minced, to taste
½ teaspoon salt

In a medium bowl, mash all of the ingredients together with a fork until blended but still chunky. Season, to taste. Refrigerate until ready to serve; it will keep about two days, but it's best served immediately. To keep it from browning too quickly in the refrigerator place plastic wrap directly on the surface. *Makes about 2 cups.*

41

NACHOS

This is another Mexican dish, and we like to fry our own tortilla chips. In a pinch, I can allow for a good store-bought chip, but the way some places do it now, where they get a basket of chips, pour fake cheese over it and toss on some chopped-up jalapeños, is *not* a nacho. A real nacho is an individual chip with real grated cheese and a pepper. When you do it right, it's really a wonderful hors d'oeuvre: spicy and tangy and really good. It's important, though, not to do the big piles of stuff. These are individual chips laid out and you might have two or three bites in a good chip; it's not something you just pop into your mouth. These are great with a big group and go well with a cold beer or a Mesquite-a-Rita (page 27).

6 corn tortillas, cut into quarters
Oil
½ cup grated cheddar cheese
1 jalapeño, pickled or fresh, diced
Pico de Gallo (page 40)

Fry the corn tortillas in a skillet with a little oil until crispy. Place the chips flat on a baking sheet and cover with grated cheese and top with diced jalapeño, to taste. Broil in the oven for 4 to 5 minutes, or until the cheese melts. After removing from the oven, top with a spoonful of Pico de Gallo (page 40) for a fresh, crisp taste. Salt, if desired. *Makes 24 nachos.*

SHRIMP DIP

This has a little spice to it, but the creaminess cuts it just enough. And the shrimp has that refreshing flavor, so it's ideal for warm weather. And if you love seafood, you can substitute crab or lobster (but remember to add the seafood last so it doesn't get too broken up).

2 8-ounce packages cream cheese
8 ounces sour cream
8 ounces Picante Sauce (page 45)
1 bunch green onions, chopped
1 pound cooked shrimp, peeled and deveined, diced

Blend the cream cheese and sour cream, then stir in the picante sauce and chopped green onions. Add the shrimp to mixture. Refrigerate immediately and serve chilled with crackers.
Serves 20.

PICANTE SAUCE

This is a much smoother salsa than the Pico de Gallo (page 40). You pour it over something rather than scooping it on. It's become a really popular condiment in recent years, in part, I think, because it's low in calories. I've even seen people put it on a baked potato, and we joke about it putting ketchup out of business.

Red Picante:
1 large onion, chopped
1 tablespoon cooking oil
2 large ripe tomatoes, peeled and
  coarsely chopped, should yield 2 cups
3–6 jalapeños, finely chopped
1–3 cloves garlic, minced
1/2 teaspoon salt

Sauté the onion in oil until clear; do not brown. Add remaining ingredients and simmer for 20 to 30 minutes.

Green Picante:
1 large onion, chopped
1 tablespoon cooking oil
2 pounds fresh tomatillos OR 4 10-ounce cans, drained
3 large green or poblano chiles,
  chopped
2 cloves garlic, minced
6–8 fresh jalapeños OR serranos

Sauté the onion until clear; do not brown. Add the remaining ingredients and simmer for 20 to 30 minutes.
Makes approximately 4 cups.

CHILE CON QUESO

This is a real Texas staple, but I like ours because of the sausage, which is a little different than your standard recipe. It gives it a thicker consistency, so with a fried chip it really stands up. With most everything I do, I like to use fresh, homemade ingredients, but with queso, you just can't beat Velveeta. Again, this is an easy party recipe and can be doubled and tripled to accommodate your numbers, but it's important to keep it on a warmer because you don't want it to solidify.

1 pound hot or mild pork sausage
½ onion, chopped
2 pounds Velveeta cheese
1 12-ounce can tomatoes & green chiles
7 ounces green chiles, chopped

Sauté the sausage and onion together in a skillet until done; drain away excess grease. Melt the Velveeta slowly over low heat and add tomatoes and chiles. This dip needs to be served in a chafing dish and kept hot. Serve with crisp tortilla chips. Leftovers can be frozen and reheated. *Serves 20.*

Settling the Dust (LS Cowboys Drinking at a Bar) Old Tascosa, Texas; *Erwin E. Smith, photographer; nitrate negative, ca. 1907; courtesy Texas and Southwestern Cattle Raisers Foundation, Fort Worth, Texas, and Amon Carter Museum, Fort Worth, Texas.*

47

REFRIED BEAN DIP

This is a simple dish, but it's tasty and a great way to use leftover beans.

2 cups cooked Ranch Beans (page 155)
¼ cup Picante Sauce (page 45)
1 cup grated Monterey Jack OR longhorn cheese
1–2 jalapeños, seeded and chopped, to taste
¼ teaspoon ground cumin
1½ teaspoons chopped cilantro

Mash the beans or purée in a food processor. Mix in the remaining ingredients. Place in an ovenproof container. Heat in the oven at 350° until thoroughly warmed. May also be heated in the microwave oven. Serve with crisp tortilla chips. *Serves 10 to 12.*

JALAPEÑO BITES

These are the first things we run out of when we cater a big party. The cream cheese really takes some of the fire out of the jalapeños, but it's important to make sure the bacon gets done. I like to finish these on the grill just to add a nice smoky flavor.

6 jalapeños, fresh or pickled, cut in half lengthwise
   and seeded
3 ounces cream cheese, softened
4 slices uncooked bacon, cut into thirds

Preheat oven to 350°. Stuff each jalapeño half with the cream cheese and wrap with a bacon piece. Place on a baking sheet with cream cheese side up, secure with a toothpick and bake until bacon is done. These can also be done on a closed grill. *Makes 12 bites.*

PICKLED OKRA

Pickled okra is wonderful at a cocktail party. It's crisp and cold and sharp, and, unlike cooked okra, it doesn't have what we call "the slime factor." It's also a garnish for the Cowboy Bloody Mary (page 28) or a summer salad. They're a little spicy, but nothing overpowering.

4 pounds okra (small okra pods, little finger-sized, are best)
1 pound fresh jalapeño or serrano peppers,
   sliced into thin rounds
4 cups white vinegar
4 cups water
10–12 plump garlic cloves, peeled and thinly sliced
12–24 sprigs of fresh dill OR heads of dill blossoms
½ cup salt
¼ cup whole mustard seeds

Wash and trim the okra, leaving ½ inch of the stem on each pod as a handle. Neatly pack the okra pods vertically into sterilized jars. Slice the peppers into rounds and add to the jars of okra. Combine the remaining ingredients in a large sauce pan and bring to a boil; pour over the okra and peppers. Seal.

TEXAS BRUSCHETTA WITH SOURDOUGH BREAD CHIPS

This is our answer to the Italian hors d'oeuvre that's so popular in restaurants from New York to Los Angeles. I use good sourdough in a lot of things because I love the texture—I just don't like smooth breads—and it stands up when you're cooking it. You can even serve them on their own or with a little Parmesan cheese.

Sourdough Breadchips:
¾ cup olive oil
3–4 cloves garlic, finely minced
2 tablespoons finely minced fresh parsley
   OR 1 tablespoon dried
2 tablespoons finely minced fresh oregano
   OR 1 tablespoon dried
1 teaspoon freshly ground black pepper
½ teaspoon salt
1 sourdough baguette, sliced ¼ inch thick

Pico de Gallo (page 40) OR Roasted Red
   Pepper Sauce (page 94)

Preheat oven to 300°. Mix together the olive oil, garlic, herbs and spices. Spread each bread slice with a little of the oil mixture. Arrange the slices on a baking sheet and bake for about 15 minutes until slices just begin to brown. Turn once during cooking to brown both sides. When they emerge from the oven, top with a spoonful of "Pico" or Roasted Red Pepper Sauce.

Store unused chips in a tightly closed container to preserve freshness. *Serves 8.*

ON THE WAGON

The primary feature is the chuck box, often made to a cook's specifications, with cupboards, drawers, shelves and enough hooks to hold just about everything the cook might need for a meal, and then some. He has everything at his fingertips, which generally includes:

Salt
Flour
Beans
Sugar
Molasses
Coffee
Lard
Canned goods
Dried fruit
Bacon and fresh beef,
    wrapped in tarps
Spices
Tableware
Some basic medical supplies
The coffee grinder, nailed
    to the side of the wagon
A knife rack
A "business drawer"
    for important documents
Toolbox
A cowhide harness, or "coonie,"
    hung between the axles to
    carry firewood
Water barrels, strapped to the
    sideboards
The bottom cupboard, or
    "boot," to hold crocks, Dutch
    ovens, skillets and stewpots
Extra horseshoes
A shoeing outfit
Branding irons
A stack of bedrolls
A protective canvas sheet to
    pull across the wagon's bows

TEXAS PICKLED SHRIMP

This is what happens when the spirit of Texas cooking gets a hold of some beautiful seafood from the Gulf Coast.

2 pounds peeled and deveined raw shrimp
2 medium onions, sliced
1½ cups salad oil
1½ cups vinegar
¼ cup sugar
1½ teaspoons salt
¼ cup capers, with juice
1 tablespoon plus 1 teaspoon crushed red pepper
6–8 splashes of Tabasco

Place the shrimp in boiling salted water, turn off heat and let stand, covered, 3 to 5 minutes, or until pink and tender. Drain and rinse with cold water. Chill. Alternate layers of shrimp and sliced onion rings in a sealable container. Mix the remaining ingredients and pour over shrimp and onions. Chill for 6 hours or more, shaking or inverting occasionally. Remove the shrimp from marinade and serve. *Serves about 6 to 8 as an appetizer.*

HOT CRAB SPREAD

Courtesy of the Hawkins Ranch (page 182), this is a favorite for anyone with a crab wharf outside their back door.

8 ounces cream cheese
1 tablespoon milk
½ pound fresh crabmeat, picked over for shells
2 tablespoons finely chopped onion
½ teaspoon prepared horseradish
¼ teaspoon salt
Dash of pepper
⅓ cup toasted pecans OR sliced almonds

Preheat oven to 375°. Mix all the ingredients except the nuts. Spoon into an ovenproof baking dish and sprinkle with the pecans or almonds. Bake for 15 minutes and serve with assorted crackers. *Serves 8 to 10.*

Will Rogers at the Stamford, Texas, Cowboy Reunion; *photographer unknown; ca.1930; courtesy Swenson Land and Cattle Company archives.*

BOILED SHRIMP

This is something Texans love and it comes from the early ranches along the Gulf Coast. Of course, you wouldn't find shrimp on a cattle drive or even at the cookshack on inland ranches, but at places like the Hawkins and King ranches, seafood is right outside their back door. Fresh shrimp with Red Sauce (opposite page) is also a natural complement to beef; it's just a nice crisp, cold taste.

2 pounds peeled and deveined large shrimp*
1 box shrimp boil
1 gallon water

Boil the shrimp boil and water (remember not to open the packet of shrimp boil, submerse the entire packet). Add the shrimp and reduce heat. Cook until shrimp are pink and begin to curl (3 to 5 minutes). Drain the shrimp and leave in colander. Place the colander in a bed of ice and your shrimp will chill quickly. You will need to change the ice frequently. *Serves 10 to 12.*

*Large shrimp are approximately 16 to 20 shrimp per pound.

GRILLED SHRIMP

These shrimp are marvelous hot off the grill and served with informal cocktails.

1½ pounds large shrimp
  (16–20 shrimp per pound)
1 cup vegetable oil
Juice of 3–4 lemons
2 cloves garlic
2 bay leaves
½ teaspoon salt

Peel the shrimp, leaving tails on. Butterfly the shrimp by making a cut along the top and splitting each one open. Place in a glass bowl.

Combine the oil, lemon juice, garlic, bay leaves and salt, and pour over the shrimp. Marinate 2 to 4 hours in the refrigerator, stirring occasionally.

Grill over very hot coals, 4 to 6 inches from the heat, for 3 to 4 minutes per side, depending on the size of the shrimp. Baste with the remaining marinade. *Serves 4.*

RED SAUCE

7 ounces ketchup
¼ teaspoon salt
¼ teaspoon black pepper
½ tablespoon prepared horseradish
¼ teaspoon Tabasco
½ teaspoon Worcestershire sauce

Combine all the ingredients and serve. *Makes 1 cup.*

ROASTED PECANS

If you're looking for something to serve with a couple of drinks, these are great. We Texans are blessed with a generous allotment of native pecan trees. They grow on riverbanks and you can go down there and pick them, come home and toast them up in the oven, and they make a wonderful snack or topping. It is a Christmas tradition on ranches around here to give little bags of them as gifts.

2 cups pecan halves
2 tablespoons melted butter
Seasoning salt, if desired

Preheat oven to 250°. In a small bowl, toss the pecans lightly in melted butter, then spread them out evenly on a baking sheet. Roast the pecans in the oven for approximately 30 to 45 minutes, or until you begin to smell the pecans. Watch carefully—they can brown quickly. *Serves 8.*

If using as an appetizer or a snack, sprinkle lightly with seasoned salt. If you are using the roasted pecans in a recipe or a salad, do not salt.

PICADILLO FOR CHILE RELLENOS OR HOLIDAY DIPPING

This lightly sweet, spicy picadillo is often used as the stuffing for holiday Chiles Rellenos—Mexican stuffed peppers.

2 pounds ground beef
1 large onion, chopped
1 tablespoon olive oil
3 cloves garlic, minced
1 pound mushrooms, sliced or chopped
2 red bell peppers, seeded and chopped
1 poblano pepper, red or green, chopped
1 pound ripe fresh tomatoes, chopped OR 1 16-ounce can diced tomatoes
1 8-ounce can tomato sauce
1 cup raisins
3 tablespoons vinegar
1 teaspoon sugar or honey
1 teaspoon salt
1 tablespoon chili powder
1 teaspoon ground cumin
1 teaspoon ground cinnamon
½ teaspoon ground cloves
1 cup broken or coarsely chopped pecans
Several sprigs fresh cilantro, snipped or chopped, if available

Sauté the beef and onions in oil until onions are soft and beef is browned. Add garlic, mushrooms, peppers, tomatoes, tomato sauce, raisins and vinegar. Stir to combine well and simmer 15 minutes. Add sugar, salt and spices, and simmer for an additional 15 to 30 minutes to blend flavors well. (May be refrigerated at this point until serving time.) To serve, add the pecans, reheat quickly, remove from heat and add a handful of chopped cilantro. *Serves 8.*

BLACK BEAN AND ROASTED CORN SALAD

The black bean is a Mexican influence but this is also a traditional Texas summer salad. And it's such a nice looking salad—with all the colors—that I like to serve it as a first course before a beef dinner.

3 cups cooked black beans
3 ears roasted yellow corn, cut from the cob
1 medium red bell pepper, seeded and diced
1 cup thinly sliced green onions (tops and bottoms)
2 cloves garlic, finely chopped
1 tablespoon chopped cilantro (optional)
1 cup Vinaigrette (below)

Vinaigrette:
⅔ cup oil
⅛ cup vinegar
½ teaspoon salt
½ teaspoon black pepper
½ teaspoon Dijon mustard

Combine the dressing ingredients and shake well. Rinse and drain the black beans. Cut roasted corn from cob trying not to break apart all the kernels. Mix together and add the pepper, green onions, garlic, cilantro and Vinaigrette. Stir again and drain before serving. (Remember not to overuse the cilantro—the taste is strong.) *Serves 8.*

TEXAS CAVIAR

This is a real Texas mainstay because black-eyed peas are in everybody's garden. And fresh from the garden they're delicious, especially with catfish for dinner. Try serving this in a hollowed tomato half.

2 pounds shelled black-eyed peas, cooked
   OR 4 cups cooked—frozen, dried or canned
½ cup chopped green onions (tops and bottoms)
½ cup diced purple onion
1 cup diced tomato
2 cloves fresh garlic, minced
1 medium jalapeño, seeded and diced
¾ cup vegetable oil
¼ cup vinegar
1 teaspoon chopped fresh oregano
   OR ½ teaspoon dried
1 teaspoon chopped fresh basil
   OR ½ teaspoon dried
½ teaspoon salt
½ teaspoon freshly ground black pepper

57

Rinse and drain the black-eyed peas. Add the onions, tomatoes, garlic and jalapeño. Cover with the oil and vinegar and seasonings and mix thoroughly. Refrigerate immediately and let marinate for at least 6 hours, stirring occasionally. Drain marinade and serve chilled. *Serves 10.*

COOK'S GARDEN

Outside every ranch cookshack there's a garden, and this is where much of the produce eaten inside originates. In the old days you couldn't just run into town everyday, so a gar-

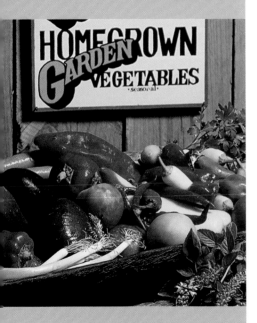

den was necessary. I've got one right in front of the restaurant and it contributes a lot. For our Sunday lunch I'll fix all vegetables out of the garden. One year we had so many cucumbers that we were giving two to every customer before they even ordered. There's something about a garden that just makes food taste better.

POTATO SALAD

This is just standard Texas barbecue fare. You have brisket, maybe some chicken and sausage or ribs, and your fixings; and this is your main fixing.

2 pounds red or white boiling potatoes
¼ cup olive oil
2 tablespoons vinegar
1 teaspoon prepared mustard
2 green onions with 2 inches green tops, finely sliced
1 tablespoon chopped fresh parsley
½ teaspoon salt
½ teaspoon freshly ground black pepper

Boil the potatoes until tender but still firm, about 20 minutes. Slice and toss with the oil, vinegar, mustard, green onions, parsley, salt and pepper. *Serves 8.*

Variation:
2 pounds red or white boiling potatoes
½ cup homemade Texas Mayonnaise (page 125)
1 teaspoon prepared mustard
3 hard-boiled eggs, chopped
½ cup chopped onion
2 stalks celery, chopped
½ teaspoon salt
½ teaspoon freshly ground black pepper

Boil the potatoes until tender but still firm, about 20 minutes. Drain the potatoes, peel if you wish, and dice. Gently mix with the mayonnaise, mustard, chopped eggs, onions, celery, salt and pepper. Refrigerate until serving time. *Serves 8.*

COTTAGE CHEESE SALAD

I grew up with this salad. It's my great-grandmother's old Texas recipe. She settled here in the early days of Abilene. She died when I was young, but I remember my grandmother making it and talking about her. If you like cottage cheese, which I do, it's a great snack to have around. I make it and put it in the refrigerator, and then when I'm looking for a snack, I'll just go in and get a big bowl. Try serving it on a slice of fresh tomato.

16 ounces cottage cheese (small curd)
$\frac{1}{2}$ cup chopped green onions (tops and bottoms)
$\frac{1}{2}$ cup chopped pecans
1 clove garlic, minced
Coarsely ground black pepper and salt, to taste

Combine all the ingredients and refrigerate. Serve chilled. Will keep for several days. *Serves 6 to 8.*

AUTUMN FRUIT SALAD

This is our take on the Waldorf salad. It's a great way to use fresh fruit, and the homemade mayonnaise is a real Texas touch. It's very simple and very refreshing, but it's a salad you really need to make and serve immediately, because even though you've added lemon juice, the fruit does brown. Of course, all fruits need to be rinsed thoroughly. Use firm pears with a nice skin. These will hold up better in the salad.

60

4 red Delicious apples with peels, cored
2 green pears with peels, cored
Juice of 1 lemon
¼ pound red seedless grapes
¼ pound green seedless grapes
⅓ cup homemade Texas Mayonnaise (page 125)
1 tablespoon sugar
1 cup chopped pecans

Chop the apples and pears into bite-sized pieces and mix together. Squeeze the lemon juice over the fruit to prevent browning. Stir in the grapes. Mix together the mayonnaise and sugar. Toss the fruit in the mayonnaise mixture and top with the pecans. *Serves 6.*

COLESLAW

Coleslaw is almost always served with barbecue. I've even been known to add chunks of fresh pineapple, which just makes it that much more refreshing in the summertime.

1 medium head cabbage, cored
  and sliced or shredded finely
1 tablespoon grated sweet onion
1 fresh carrot, grated
1 cup homemade Texas Mayonnaise (page 125)
¼ cup white vinegar
1 tablespoon sugar
Salt and pepper, to taste

Stir all the ingredients together and serve as soon as possible, while the cabbage is still crisp. *Serves 6 to 8.*

61

PERINI RANCH SALAD

Romaine and green leaf lettuces have completely different textures and tastes, and we throw in some iceberg for the crunch. This is a very simple, plain, crisp salad.

½ head green leaf lettuce
½ head romaine lettuce
½ head iceberg lettuce
¼ cup mushrooms
20 cherry tomatoes
½ red onion, sliced
6–8 green onions, for garnish

Dressing:
1 cup buttermilk
1 cup homemade Texas Mayonnaise (page 125)
1 large clove garlic, finely minced
1–2 scallions, with 2 inches of green top, thinly sliced
1 teaspoon finely minced fresh parsley
   OR ½ teaspoon dried parsley
1 teaspoon finely minced oregano
   OR ½ teaspoon dried oregano
½ teaspoon ground black pepper
½ teaspoon salt

Combine the dressing ingredients in a large jar. Shake vigorously to combine thoroughly. If time permits, refrigerate for 30 minutes to allow flavors to blend before serving time. Toss the salad ingredients with the dressing. *Serves 6 to 8.*

SALPICON

This is a delicious meat salad that can actually be served hot or cold.

3 cups sliced or shredded leftover pot roast or roast beef
1/2 cup Vinaigrette (page 56)
3/4 cup chopped green chiles OR poblano
  OR Anaheim peppers
1/4 pound Monterey Jack cheese, grated
2 avocados, peeled and sliced
Chopped fresh cilantro, to taste
2 tablespoons chopped fresh parsley
1 chopped fresh jalapeño

Mix the beef with Vinaigrette and marinate overnight. Top the beef with the chopped green chiles and cheese. Then layer with the avocado slices and sprinkle on the cilantro and chopped parsley and jalapeño. Serve chilled.

To serve warm, bake at 325° for 20 to 30 minutes, until meat is thoroughly heated. *Serves 16 to 20.*

63

Frank Smith Watering His Horse. Cross-B Ranch, Crosby County, Texas; *Erwin E. Smith, photographer; glass plate negative; ca. 1909; courtesy Texas and Southwestern Cattle Raisers Foundation, Fort Worth, Texas, and Amon Carter Museum, Fort Worth, Texas.*

CHUCKWAGON BEEF SALAD WITH HOT BACON DRESSING

This is a real meal in itself, if you're not too hungry but want some meat. I think it makes a great lunch. We ate this all the time when I was growing up, with leftover steak.

1 pound top sirloin, cut 1 inch thick
½ teaspoon salt
1 teaspoon coarsely ground black pepper
1 teaspoon fresh oregano OR ½ teaspoon dried
1 teaspoon fresh basil OR ½ teaspoon dried
1 teaspoon fresh oregano OR ½ teaspoon dried
1 teaspoon fresh parsley OR ½ teaspoon dried
8 cups washed and torn romaine lettuce
1 red bell pepper, seeded and halved
1 onion, sliced into thick rounds

Dressing:
4 strips bacon, fried crisp (reserve drippings)
1 tablespoon flour
½ cup water
½ cup vinegar
2 tablespoons sugar
Salt and pepper, to taste

To make the dressing, add flour to bacon drippings, over medium heat, stirring to dissolve. Add water, vinegar and sugar, stirring constantly. Cook to thicken. Add salt and pepper, to taste. Crumble bacon and add to the dressing.

Season the steak with salt, pepper and herbs. Grill the steak, red peppers and onions 4 to 6 inches from medium coals, 12 to 15 minutes (for medium rare), turning once.

Slice the steak diagonally into ¼-inch-thick strips. Slice the red pepper into thin strips. Arrange the steak, peppers and onions over lettuce. Serve with warmed dressing. *Serves 4.*

LISA'S FAVORITE CAESAR SALAD

This salad has intense flavors and is terrific served with your favorite steak.

65

Dressing:
6 tablespoons olive oil
6 cloves garlic, chopped
1 teaspoon dry mustard
1 teaspoon coarsely ground black pepper
1 teaspoon salt
3 teaspoons capers with juice
3 anchovies, chopped and drained
2 tablespoons tarragon vinegar
2 tablespoons fresh lemon juice

1 head romaine lettuce, rinsed and drained
1/3 cup grated Parmesan cheese
2 cups sourdough croutons

Combine the dressing ingredients. Mix thoroughly. Toss with chilled romaine lettuce and sprinkle with freshly grated Parmesan and sourdough croutons. *Serves 6.*

Hint: The Texas Sourdough Bruschetta (page 49) makes an excellent crouton, just use smaller pieces of bread.

PITCHFORK RANCH

Straddling King and Dickens counties, the ranch was established in 1870 on a bond of friendship. Boyhood pals from Mississippi, D. B. Gardner and Eugene F. Williams bought a herd of cattle bearing the Pitchfork brand and began accumulating land. Today, operations are handled by a manager; Bob Moorhouse (whom we have to thank for the spectacular ranch photographs in these pages) has run things since 1986. The Pitchfork chuck wagon earns praise both in regular competitions and from the cowboys it serves during roundup.

Everyday a bell is rung at 11:45. The cowboys arrive at the cookshack to overturned plates

Pitchfork ★ Ranch

at each setting and only sit down when the second bell tolls at exactly noon. In observance of strict cowboy etiquette, all hats are left on the porch. In the communal spirit of ranch life, each cowboy washes his own dish after lunch. The favorite meal around the Pitchfork, according to Bob, is chicken-fried steak, ranch beans, mashed potatoes and gravy.

CUCUMBER AND ONION SALAD

On a recent trip to the Pitchfork Ranch, we had this salad with lunch.

2 pounds slender cucumbers with skins
   (preferably seedless), sliced ¼ inch thick
1 large Texas sweet onion, thinly sliced
2 cups vinegar
½ cup sugar
2 teaspoons salt
2 cups ice cubes
Parsley and cilantro, to taste (optional)

Combine the vinegar, sugar and salt, and add ice cubes. Stir in herbs. Toss cucumbers and onions in dressing and refrigerate. Let sit in refrigerator at least 30 minutes before serving time. *Serves 8.*

PICKLED BEETS

These are a great side with lunch, and when used as a garnish they add beautiful color.

3 cups sliced beets, cooked
2 cups vinegar
1 cup water
½ cup sugar
1 teaspoon ground allspice
6 whole cloves
3 sticks cinnamon

Put the beets into a quart jar. Boil the vinegar, water, sugar and spices for 5 minutes, cool slightly and pour over beets. Cover and store in the refrigerator. Pickle overnight. *Makes one quart. Serves 8.*

AVOCADO AND GRAPEFRUIT SALAD

When the avocado is fresh, this is a fantastic summertime salad. Texas is known for our Ruby Red grapefruits.

Dressing:
1 cup oil
1 tablespoon Dijon mustard
1/2 cup sugar
1/4 cup poppy seeds
1/2 teaspoon salt
1/4 cup vinegar
1 head romaine lettuce

2 avocados, peeled and sliced
3 Ruby Red grapefruits, sectioned
  and membranes removed
1 small red onion, sliced into thin rings

Combine the dressing ingredients in a jar with a lid, and shake well.

Tear the lettuce into bite-sized pieces and make a bed for the fruit. Place the avocado and grapefruit on the lettuce. Lightly toss with dressing. Place the onion rings on top of the salad for extra color and flavor. Serve immediately. *Serves 6 to 8.*

BEEF AND OTHER MAIN DISHES

BEEF AND OTHER MAIN DISHES

There's a real mystique surrounding beef, and particularly steak. It's a standard, the top of the line. You just don't say, "Let's go out for a chicken breast." People eat steak on special occasions, and I'm lucky to get to host people coming for just those kinds of celebrations. We have lots of local people who we see every now and again, but when their aunt comes in from California, or Alaska, or somebody comes in from Japan, this is where they come. This is Texas, so they don't go to the sushi bar—and I love sushi. It's like when I was in Durango, Colorado, and I went to a restaurant that did not have rainbow trout. They had mahi mahi and exotic things like that, and I'm sure they were good, but when I'm in the mountains I want some trout. When you go to the coast, you eat seafood.

In Texas, we raise a lot of cattle, so naturally, we eat a lot of beef. Traditionally, ranchers always kept a few cattle on feed at the ranch. The cowboys didn't get paid much but they did get a place to live, a pickup

Left: Grilled Sirloin Steak (page 81).

71

and about half a beef every six months or so. So ranchers always had their own beef. The freezer business used to be huge because everyone had a chest freezer in the back room that was just filled with beef. Now if you want a steak, you just run to the store and buy one steak.

At the restaurant, we cut all our own meat and only season with our rubs. That's the great thing about beef, it doesn't need some fancy preparation to be delicious. Our seasonings are simple and just enough to really awaken the flavors of the meat. And that's the way good beef should be eaten. These recipes range from practically just throwing a steak on the fire to something that might take a couple of hours, but they're all worth trying. Most are standard ranch or chuckwagon fare, but many may seem just as appropriate on a white linen tablecloth. And, of course, some may not.

       We did Watt Matthews's Princeton class of '21 reunion party in 1989. There were only about 25 of them left in the class, but they were CEOs of big companies and all sorts of important people. Watt wanted an authentic ranch party, so he asked us to fix a steer's head, which is a traditional cowboy dish, but I'd never done it. In fact, I'd never even seen it. The only reference I had was the movie *Giant*. In the movie, Elizabeth Taylor faints at the sight. We knew it was roasted in the ground, so we just sort of figured it out. We left it in this underground oven for like 18 hours. When it came time to pull this thing out of the ground, of course I had all these old Princeton guys watching me, and I had to play like this was an everyday event, and I'd never done it before in my life. So we got it out, unwrapped it and set it on the table. And I remembered in the movie that they broke it open and served straight from the natural serving dish— and so did I, in front of this big audience. People came through the line and I served them up slices of meat and scoops of pit

73

ALL STEAKS ARE NOT EQUAL

Know which cut is best for your needs. Some can just be thrown on the grill while others need to be cut a specific way or marinated. Sirloin is great for backyard grilling for the family, but if you've got company coming over, cook some ribeyes. And when in doubt, consult your butcher.

The bite, or tooth, is a term for the texture and consistency of a piece of meat, or your experience biting into it. The most naturally tender beef I've come across is Kobe beef in Japan. It's very expensive and so very tender. These animals are so coddled, I've been told the cowboys actually go out and massage the animals on a regular basis.

roasted brains, acting like I do this all the time. Then this one lady came along and said, "I'm sorry, but I just can't eat that."

And I said, "I understand," and she walked right by me and got a whole big plate of Calf Fries (see page 38). I just didn't have the heart to tell her.

ON THE GRILL

Remember, on the chuck wagon, the heat source is wood, and most of our cooking comes from that—something grilled over a wood fire. That's not just Texan; whether you're in Tuscany or Argentina or whatever, it's a traditional method of cooking.

At the restaurant we use mesquite because it's native Texas wood, and there's a lot of it in this area. We used to pull it all off the ranch but now we go through so much of it that we have it delivered 20 cords at a time. We use wood that's probably 10 years old and it has to be good and dry mesquite so that the tar or pitch that is naturally in the wood is gone. And we cook with the coals, which means we take a pile of mesquite, burn it down to coals and then shovel the coals underneath the grill. But the mesquite wood makes a good hot, even-burning coal, so you don't get as many hot spots as you might with other woods. Other parts of the country use other hardwoods like oak or hickory, but we use mesquite

because we have it right outside the back door. Unfortunately, there probably aren't too many people out there with a mesquite-burning barbecue pit in their backyard. So if you are using regular charcoal, try sprinkling some mesquite or other hardwood chips on top of the coals. You won't get the same amount of heat as with the mesquite but you will get some of the flavor. Mesquite chips can be found in grocery stores nationwide.

What determines the method of cooking is the height of the meat above the coals. If you're cooking a steak you want it on a grill right above the coals, and I believe in cooking a steak with a little bit of flame, because you don't want a gray steak. We keep it hot enough so it sears the outside of the steak, and gives good grill marks and a little char, which adds a tremendous amount of flavor. This really complements the flavor of your beef. Before you throw anything on the grill, get the fire hot enough to where you can't keep your palm a couple of inches from the grill for more than a few seconds.

75

Opposite page:
Dale Cronk, Head
Cook, Perini Ranch
Steakhouse.

Swenson Ranch managers and cowboys with Swede Swenson at lower left, and A. J. Swenson at upper left; *photographer unknown; ca. 1920; courtesy Swenson Land and Cattle Company archives.*

Clean your grill with a wire brush and then, once it gets hot, oil it with a little vegetable oil or steak fat. And let your steaks reach room temperature before putting them on the fire; cold meats will really stick to a hot grill, but after cooking a bit it will release some. So don't feel like you have to tear it off as soon as it starts to stick. And use a pair of tongs or a spatula to flip it because you don't want to puncture it with a fork.

We cut our steaks a good inch and a half thick, so they average 16 ounces. Then we have a mixture of seasonings—our rub—that we put on both sides before grilling. It's not a big project, no need to marinate for hours, just rub them and put them on the fire. You only need to turn a steak once; don't stand out there playing with it because you have nothing else to do. Put it on a real hot fire and leave it alone for a couple of minutes. Then it's just a question of how long to cook.

On the trail, they might cook meat pretty well done so it would keep, but when you cook a good steak beyond medium you're really jeopardizing the quality of the steak—because you cook the juices out and that's where the flavor is, and you're also making it tougher. I personally like my steak medium rare to, well, raw, if the circumstances call for it. I'll build a fire at the house and end up eating half the steak with salt, pepper and a little onion before the coals are even ready. In Italy, they call that carpaccio. But honestly, I think the American public overcooks their meat, and it's a shame because they miss out on a wonderful steak and wonder why it's tough and doesn't have any flavor, or they blame the cut or they think they don't know how to do it. A steak should be at least an inch and a quarter thick, because that'll allow enough time to get some good color on both sides without affecting the inside.

77

HANGOVER TEMPERATURE

It's important to remember that all meat has a hangover or carryover temperature, and the bigger the cut the more the hangover temperature. I mean that a steak doesn't stop cooking as soon as you pull it off the grill. It retains a lot of heat and takes a little while to cool

down. Of course, a steak that's an inch and a half thick will cool down fast, compared to a big 14-pound roast. So you want to take it off a little before it's really ready. I think a lot of people cook a piece of meat until it reaches the desired temperature, take it out and say, "boy, everything's fine," and then cut into it a half hour later and it's well done. They think they overcooked it but they didn't, they just didn't take the hangover temperature into account.

I'll never forget, when I was seven years old, sitting in the cookshack at Lambshead ranch with my father, while Watt Matthews was cooking some steaks. My father turned to me and said, "Now Tom, this is going to be very rare and you have to chew it up or you'll choke." Now every time I get very rare meat, which, of course, I love now, I think of that night.

We often use a meat thermometer in roasting our larger cuts and have done it enough times to pretty well know when a steak is the doneness we want. However, I recommend the touch method. This takes some getting used to because you really want to become familiar with the firmness of the degree of doneness that you like, but when you do, it never fails. Before putting your steak on the fire, touch it and notice how soft it is. As it cooks it gets a lot firmer and you need to be touching it every so often until it gets where you want it. Obviously this is only perfected after much trial and error, so if you have to, you can cut into it. Now I don't recommend this because you do lose some of your juices, but I'd rather you do that than overcook it. And don't be tempted to put the top on the grill. You might think that you're trapping heat and cooking more thoroughly, but you're cutting off air to the fire, which lowers its temperature and slows the cooking.

The author, right, with Watt Matthews, Lambshead Ranch, 1975; *photograph courtesy Tom Perini.*

FISH, GAME AND POULTRY: HUNTING AND GATHERING

Not everybody eats beef with every meal— even in Texas. We're open-minded; it's just a real steak and potatoes kind of place. But there are plenty of beautiful nonmeat dishes made from the Lone Star State's bounty that are as natural to Texas as the longhorn.

Even on a cattle drive, eating beef was not necessarily something that happened everyday. A team of cowboys was given a certain number of cattle, and those animals had to be accounted for when they got where they were going. The more you ate the less you had to sell, and losing a couple of dozen cattle didn't sit real well with the people paying you to drive them to market. I don't mean they couldn't eat any, but if they came across some wild game they were always quick to draw. Or if they passed a farm they would jump at the chance to trade a hindquarter for some chicken or eggs or even vegetables.

79

CUTS OF STEAK

RIBEYE

The ribeye is a steak with quite a bit of marbling and it happens to be my personal favorite. It's really the same cut as the prime rib, only it's cut into steaks and then grilled, instead of roasted, then sliced. It's a wonderful cut for grilling because that marbling gives it flavor and tenderness. But remember a steak is a lot thinner than a roast, so you don't want to put on so much rub that you overpower it.

FILET

The filet is cut from the tenderloin and it is the leanest cut of meat. I think of it as a dainty steak, as it's also the most tender because it's not really used as a muscle. A filet takes a little longer to cook because it's thicker, but because it's so lean it lacks the flavor of other cuts. We wrap them in bacon, or you might try them with the Roasted Garlic-Horseradish Cream (page 83). For the really well-done orders we like to butterfly them, but, again, I don't recommend you cook meat that long. Particularly with a filet, where the outside will really burn up before the inside gets done.

STRIP

The strip is a good lean cut, but you pay a price for that leanness, which is flavor. If someone is really watching their fat content this is what they ought to cook. It's cut from the top loin, and has a good bite and less marbling.

SIRLOIN

The sirloin is a larger cut with wonderful flavor due, in part, to the bone in it. It's great for grilling for the whole family in the backyard, because you can cut it into strips. Put a couple of these on the grill and cook one medium and one rare, slice them up and you can take care of everybody.

FLANK AND SKIRT

These cuts are popular these days, but they can be very fibrous and tough if not properly prepared. It's best to marinate them and then slice, across the grain, into quarter-inch slices. The marinade tenderizes the steak and also seasons it. Thanks to the *fajita*, skirt steak has become very popular. The Mexican dish used to be a great way to eat what was a pretty undesirable and so a pretty cheap cut of meat. It was practically considered a by-product of the animal, but now it's as expensive as sirloin. A skirt steak needs to be cleaned up a little: trim off the excess fat, and then soak the steak in a marinade, which helps break down the fibers. I don't recommend trying to cook either flank or skirt steak rare.

PORTERHOUSE OR T-BONE

A porterhouse is your classic cut of steak and it's like having two steaks in one. There's a bone running down the middle and on one side you have the strip and on the other side is the filet. So while there is some fat and great flavor around the bone, the steaks themselves are quite lean. The porterhouse needs to be a good thick cut: 1½ inches and up.

81

ROUND AND RUMP

Meat from the hind legs of the beef is very lean and less tender than loin and rib cuts. This means round steaks need to be cooked a little longer, but with a good marinade, they can really be delicious. They can also be a little less expensive and are great for stewing.

BEEF TENDERLOIN

5-pound beef tenderloin
Olive oil
Perini Ranch Steak Rub (page 84)

Preheat oven to 475°. Remove fat and silver skin. Brush the meat with olive oil and completely coat the tenderloin with the dry rub. Insert a meat thermometer. Place in an oven for 10 minutes at 475°; lower the oven temperature to 425° and continue cooking for about 20–25 minutes or until the thermometer reads 130° for medium rare.

Remove the tenderloin from the oven and let it stand for 10 minutes before slicing.* The key to cooking tenderloin is to be sure not to overcook it. I recommend that you slice the beef thinly and serve it with Roasted Garlic-Horseradish Cream (page 83). *Serves 12 to 16.*

Remember your hangover temperature (page 78).

ROASTED GARLIC-HORSERADISH CREAM

The perfect complement to the delicate flavor of a tenderloin.

1 head garlic
1 teaspoon olive oil
Salt, to taste
2 cups heavy cream
¼ cup prepared horseradish
⅛ teaspoon freshly ground white pepper

Preheat oven to 400°. Place the head of garlic in the center of a 10-inch-square piece of aluminum foil, coat the garlic with olive oil and season with salt. Wrap the foil around the garlic and bake until soft and brown, about an hour. Cool to room temperature.

In a saucepan over medium-low heat, bring the cream to just under a boil (watch so that it doesn't boil over). Reduce heat and simmer until reduced by ⅓, 12 to 15 minutes. Remove from heat and refrigerate for at least 20 minutes.

With a serrated knife, cut the roasted garlic in half horizontally and squeeze the paste into a bowl. Mix in the horseradish and pepper to form a smooth paste, then add the reduced cream and stir until smooth. Adjust seasonings, as needed.

Refrigerate at least 15 minutes before serving. *Makes 1½ cups.*

83

Chuck-wagon scene; *photographer unknown; courtesy Texas and Southwestern Cattle Raisers Foundation, Fort Worth, Texas.*

Rodeo scene, calf roping event, Texas Cowboy Reunion; *photographer unknown; courtesy Swenson Land and Cattle Company archives.*

RUBS

I'm a big believer in letting the flavors of the meat speak for themselves and not covering them with thick sauces or even, in most cases, marinating. I think these rubs add a little flavor but mostly they bring out the meat's natural flavors. But don't put one of these on a piece of meat and let it sit in the refrigerator overnight, because the salt will naturally pull moisture from the meat. Apply the rub and cook the meat immediately. Just remember the larger the piece of meat, the more liberal you can be with your rub. If you have a steak that's an inch and a quarter thick and you season both sides heavily, you're going to get both sides in every bite. And be sure your garlic powder is fresh—it has been known to go bad on supermarket shelves.

PERINI RANCH STEAK RUB

This is our standard rub.

1 teaspoon cornstarch OR flour
1 tablespoon salt
1 cup coarsely ground black pepper
1 teaspoon dried oregano
1 teaspoon garlic powder
1 teaspoon paprika
1 tablespoon granulated beef stock base

Mix all the ingredients together. Either sprinkle or rub into the meat. *Makes 1¼ cups.*

TEXAS HERB RUB

With the prime rib, there's a lot of outside surface and the appearance is very important, so I like to use this rub with a lot of pepper and garlic. I wet the meat a little so the seasonings will really stick and just rub it on.

1 teaspoon dried oregano leaves
1 teaspoon dried thyme leaves
1 teaspoon paprika
1 teaspoon salt
½ teaspoon garlic powder
½ teaspoon onion powder
½ teaspoon ground white pepper
½ teaspoon freshly ground black pepper
¼ teaspoon ground red pepper

Combine all the ingredients and rub over the surface of the meat.

85

BUYING AND STORING BEEF

Be sure to buy the right cut of meat for what you want to do with it. You don't want to make stew with a nice cut of steak and if you try to grill a chuck roast you'll be very disappointed. Healthy meat should really smell fresh, be slightly moist and be a shade of brownish red (not too dark). It should have some internal fat (a lot if you're going to grill it), and the external fat should be white, not yellow or brown. Also, excess liquids in

supermarket packages usually means they've been frozen and thawed at least once. Cryovaced meat, however, may appear a little darker, and have a slight odor and even some liquid (all products of the packaging process), but all these should dissipate after it's opened. A good piece of meat can keep two to three days in the refrigerator, or up to six months in the freezer, if well wrapped.

HAMBURGER

We always use ground brisket, because I like its ratio of fat to lean and its unique flavor. But ground round or chuck is also fine. We trim the excess fat, grind it ourselves, and then hand form our burgers at about half a pound each. Form it like a baseball, throwing it back and forth in your hands to make it bind. Then flatten. The Perini Ranch burger is about ¾ of an inch thick and is served with crisp bacon strips, sautéed green chiles or jalapeños, and melted cheese.

For a slightly more formal entrée, try hamburger steaks. Make the same patty and garnish with grilled onions and mushrooms and chopped green chiles. Serve on a cushion of toasted sourdough bread.

Or if you want to get really fancy, try this stuffed burger.

2 pounds ground beef
1 small onion, diced
1 tablespoon cream
1 clove garlic, crushed
½ teaspoon salt
½ teaspoon pepper
4 teaspoons Texas Barbecue Sauce (page 97)
2 tablespoons chopped jalapeños
½ cup grated cheddar cheese

Mix the beef, onion, cream, garlic, salt and pepper and form 8 thin patties. Top 4 patties with 1 teaspoon of barbecue sauce, 1 teaspoon of jalapeños and 2 tablespoons of grated cheese. Place the four remaining patties on top and press edges together to seal in fillings.

Grill over medium coals for about 6 minutes per side, turning once.

Serve on buns, or as steaks. *Makes 4 burgers.*

PARKER BURGERS

This one comes from Fess Parker and is an old family recipe.
Fess is an old friend from San Angelo who played Daniel Boone
and Davy Crockett on television and now has a vineyard in
Los Olivos California.

1 teaspoon oil
1 medium onion, finely chopped
1 red bell pepper, finely chopped
3–6 cloves garlic, minced
1½ pounds lean ground beef
1 8-ounce can tomato sauce
   OR 2 large fresh tomatoes,
   seeded and diced

3 tablespoons vinegar
3 tablespoons Worcestershire sauce
1 tablespoon fresh oregano
   OR ½ teaspoon dried oregano
½ teaspoon salt
½ teaspoon black pepper
Hot sauce or Picante Sauce (page 45), to taste
6–8 hot dog rolls

Heat the oil in a large skillet. Add the onion and pepper and
sauté, stirring frequently, until onion is softened but not browned,
about 5 minutes. Add the garlic and sauté for another minute.
Remove onion mixture from pan and set aside.

Turn up the heat under the skillet. Crumble the ground beef
into the skillet and brown. Add the onion mixture and remaining
ingredients. Simmer, stirring occa-
sionally, until the sauce is slightly
thickened and the flavors are well
blended, about 10 to 20 minutes.

While the beef is simmering, split
the rolls and toast lightly. Spoon the
meat mixture into the rolls and top
with picante, if you wish. *Serves 6.*

RANCH-ROASTED RIBEYE

This is your basic prime rib and a big piece of meat, but we put a rub on it that's heavy in black pepper and I mean we pack it on. It kind of makes a crust so when you roast it the outside is just wonderfully crisp. It's just got lots of seasoning on it and just wonderful flavors. We take it out when it's showing an internal temperature in the 120° to 125° range. Remember hangover heat (page 78). This is really an elegant cut, the kind that might be sliced at the table. It's good to serve if you're having your boss to dinner—unless, of course, you're angling for a raise.

Start with a 12-pound boneless prime rib. Trim excess fat and cover completely with lots of Ribeye Rub (opposite). Place meat on pit and roast 3 hours at 325° or until you reach an internal temperature of 125° (rare). Turn meat every hour. Remove from heat and let rest for at least 40 minutes before serving. Serve with Perini Ranch Horseradish Sauce (page 91).

RIBEYE RUB

1 cup coarsely ground salt
2 cups coarsely ground black pepper
⅓ cup flour OR corn starch
⅓ cup garlic powder
⅓ cup dried oregano

Combine all the ingredients and rub over the surface
of the meat.

LAREDO BROIL

This is our version of a traditional London Broil. It's a wonderfully tender cut when sliced thinly. It's very healthy and the
best use of round steak we know.

2½–3 pounds boneless round or top round steak,
    cut 2 to 2½ inches thick
1½ cups red wine
½ cup soy sauce
3 tablespoons Worcestershire sauce
6 cloves garlic, finely chopped
1 tablespoon freshly ground black pepper
1 tablespoon dry mustard

Marinate 24 hours in a zip-lock bag. Rub with Rib Roast Rub
(page 104) and grill over a hot fire for about 8 minutes a side.
Your meat should still be rare in the center. Let rest for about
10 minutes and slice very thinly against the grain and serve.
Serves 6 to 8.

PRIME RIB IN THE OVEN

Place roast on a wire rack in a roasting pan to keep it out of
the drippings. Preheat oven to 500° and roast for 25 minutes
to seal the juices. Reduce oven temperature to 300° and roast
to desired doneness. Use a meat thermometer to measure
internal temperature.

Tip: Plan on about 1 pound per person

IN THE OVEN

We do all our roasting in large pits and, of course, heat them with mesquite coals. It's the old style, which means that the meat is about 30 inches from the fire. Again, I don't expect many people have big roasting pits, and that's fine, because all this can be done very easily in a conventional oven. Although color and flavor always benefit from starting or finishing a roast on the grill.

I do recommend using a meat thermometer to ensure that you're cooking to the right temperature. (The new instant-read thermometers are very helpful.):

Rare: 135°
(cold red center)

Medium rare: 145°
(warm red center)

Medium: 155°
(trace of pink)

Well done: 160°
(no pink)

Also, before being carved, roasted meats need to sit a little. You don't want to cut in too soon and lose those juices that are just bursting to get out.

OVEN-ROASTED BEEF BRISKET

Brisket is the king of barbecue in the state of Texas. It's real lean on one end and then has all kinds of fat on the other, but brisket has to be cooked thoroughly or you can pull a truck with it. It used to be a real bargain cut of meat until it was discovered by the barbecuers down here that if you cook it for 14 hours, all of a sudden you get this wonderful flavor. This is a great cut for entertaining a group: It's still relatively inexpensive, fairly easy to cook and makes great leftovers.

We make a mop sauce that's ⅓ cooking oil, ⅓ water and ⅓ vinegar. We'll put in some onions, lemon, and garlic all chopped up, cook it down and then you have a mop; so when you're cooking brisket you're just mopping it on the meat.

2 tablespoons chili powder
2 tablespoons salt
1 tablespoon garlic powder
1 tablespoon onion powder
1 tablespoon ground black pepper

1 tablespoon sugar
2 teaspoons dry mustard
1 bay leaf, crushed
4 pounds beef brisket, trimmed
1½ cups Beef Stock (page 129)

Make a dry rub by combining chili powder, salt, garlic and onion powders, black pepper, sugar, dry mustard and bay leaf. Season the raw brisket on both sides with the rub. Place in a roasting pan and roast, uncovered, for one hour at 350°.

Add beef stock and enough water to yield about ½ inch of liquid in the roasting pan. Lower oven to 300°, cover pan tightly and continue cooking for 3 hours, or until fork-tender.

Trim the fat and slice meat thinly across the grain. Top with juice from the pan. *Serves 10.*

PERINI RANCH HORSERADISH SAUCE

Straight horseradish can be a little much, even for some cowboys.

2 ounces prepared horseradish
8 ounces sour cream (light may be substituted)
1 teaspoon finely chopped fresh parsley (optional)

Mix the horseradish and sour cream. Refrigerate immediately. Garnish with parsley, if desired.

Great with peppered beef tenderloin and on beef sandwiches.

TRADITIONAL POT ROAST

This falls into the category of pot cooking and you can do this on the stovetop or in the oven. At a cow camp it would probably be done in a Dutch oven.

4–5 pounds chuck roast (preferably with the bone in)
1 large onion
1½ pounds potatoes, chunked*
1 pound carrots, chopped
6 cloves garlic, chopped

Pat the roast down with the rub, sprinkle with flour and brown on all sides in hot oil. Transfer to a baking dish with some water in the bottom and bake at 350°, until the thermometer reaches your desired temperature. About an hour before beef is done, turn down heat to 275° and add the onion, potatoes, carrots and garlic. Add water, as needed. *Serves 8 to 10.*

Omit potatoes if serving with rice or noodles.

93

ROUND STEAK ROLLS

This is a classic recipe that we all grew up on.

2 pounds round steak, cut ¼ inch thick
Salt and pepper, to taste
12 slices bacon
1 cup fine breadcrumbs
1 cup grated Parmesan cheese
1 cup chopped fresh parsley
2 teaspoons basil
2 teaspoons oregano
¼ cup olive oil
2 cloves garlic, minced

String for roll-ups

Cut round steak into 4 rectangular pieces and season with salt and pepper, to taste. Layer each piece with ¼ of the bacon, breadcrumbs, cheese, parsley, basil and oregano. Starting at the wide end, roll steak and tie with string.

Heat oil in a skillet and sauté garlic until lightly browned. Sauté steak rolls for 5 minutes per side. Before serving, remove string and cut roll-ups into ½-inch slices and top with your favorite tomato sauce, if you wish.

Serve over your favorite pasta. *Serves 6.*

ROASTED RED PEPPER SAUCE

2 medium sweet red bell peppers, seeded and sliced
  OR 1 7-ounce jar of roasted red bell peppers
1 medium onion, sliced
1 tablespoon oil
1 teaspoon red wine vinegar
¼ teaspoon salt

Sauté the peppers and onion in oil until softened. Blend the pepper mixture, vinegar and salt in a blender or food processor, using pulse switch until finely chopped but not puréed (it's important that they keep some of their natural texture). *Makes 1 cup.*

MEAT LOAF

This is just good old-fashioned comfort food.

2 pounds lean ground round or chuck
1 large baking potato, grated
1 medium onion, chopped
1–2 cloves garlic (optional)
2 cups chopped fresh tomatoes OR 1 16-ounce can
    tomatoes, drained and chopped
1 red or green bell pepper, seeded and chopped
1 jalapeño, seeded and finely chopped
2 teaspoons prepared mustard OR 1 teaspoon dry mustard
1 tablespoon Worcestershire sauce
1 teaspoon salt
½ teaspoon freshly ground black pepper
1 egg, beaten
3–4 strips bacon (optional)
3–4 tablespoons Picante Sauce (page 45)
    OR tomato sauce

Mix all the ingredients, except the bacon and barbecue sauce, in
a large bowl. Form into a loaf shape in a
shallow baking pan. Top with strips of
bacon, if desired, and the picante sauce.
Bake at 350° for 1 hour. Serve with
Cowboy Potatoes (page 149).

Leftover meat loaf, sliced and grilled, makes
a great sandwich with sliced tomatoes and
cheese. *Serves 6.*

Lunchtime at the
chuck wagon; *N. H. Rose,
photographer; courtesy Texas
and Southwestern Cattle Raisers
Foundation, Fort Worth, Texas.*

95

ARMSTRONG RANCH

James Durst, a state senator in Star County, bought this South Texas ranch from Francisco Bali, the mayor of Reynosa, Mexico in 1852. The land had been part of the Beretta land grant—granted to the Bali family by the king of Spain. John Barclay Armstrong, a Texas Ranger, real estate dealer and horse trader in Austin, Texas, married Durst's daughter, Molly. Armstrong established rightful title, and stocked the ranch using the $4,000 bounty he received after capturing the outlaw John Wesley Hardin.

The midpoint of the Corpus Christi to Brownsville stage route, the Kenedy County ranch has stayed in the Armstrong

family into a second century of operation. The ranch specializes in Santa Gertrudis cattle, the first breed developed in the United States. These cattle thrive in this tropical, coastal plain.

A favorite activity for family and guests is a cookout in the shade of the spreading live oaks in the motte.

CHICKEN-FRIED STEAK

This is an honest-to-God Texas staple and we serve it every Sunday. There just aren't too many people who don't like a good chicken-fried steak, and they're real easy to find on the ranches. I like to make it with ribeye or strip because I like the bite, and I always pound it myself instead of using any kind of commercial tenderizer. I do it the old-fashioned way, where you slice it thin, pound it and fry it in the skillet, not the deep fryer. It could easily be done on the chuck wagon.

3 pounds ribeye or strip
Egg Dip (page 101)
Flour

Cut the beef about a ½ inch thick and flatten it out evenly with a mallet. Dip the steak in the egg dip, then dredge it in the flour and then repeat the process. Cover the bottom of a large skillet with about half an inch of oil and heat. When oil spatters to a few drops of water, put in your steaks. When the juices begin to surface and the bottom is nice and brown, they should be flipped and cooked until done. Serve with Cream Gravy (opposite). *Serves 8.*

CREAM GRAVY

A must with a chicken-fried steak.

3 heaping tablespoons flour
2 cups cold milk
Salt and pepper, to taste

After frying the steak, let the drippings sit until the excess browned bits of seasoning settle to the bottom of the skillet, then pour off most of the oil, leaving about 4 tablespoons and the brown bits. Add flour, stirring until well mixed. Place skillet over heat and slowly add the cold milk, stirring constantly. Cook until gravy boils. (You may need more or less milk for your desired consistency.) Salt and pepper, to taste. Serve with Chicken Fried Steak (opposite).

This is also fantastic on homemade Buttermilk Biscuits (page 141), The Judge's Fried Chicken (page 105) or on mashed potatoes.
Makes 2 cups.

BBQ SAUCE FOR BEEF

My favorite sauce.

½ cup tomato sauce
½ cup butter (1 stick)
2 tablespoons molasses
¼ cup vinegar
¼ cup strong coffee
½ teaspoon Worcestershire sauce
½ teaspoon garlic powder
½ teaspoon chili powder
½ teaspoon salt
½ teaspoon pepper

Combine ingredients and bring to a gentle boil for a few minutes. Reduce heat and simmer for 10 minutes. Serve with sliced beef.
Makes 1½ cups.

AGING BEEF

You might think beef is aged with some scientific technique that keeps any of it from going bad, but it's actually just left in the refrigerator to ripen. With dry aging, the meat is hung for an average of 21 days in a big cooler where "natural tenderizing" occurs: The enzymes

break down the muscle fibers and tissue, and actual bacteria helps break down the sinew. A good bit of the meat is lost (up to 50 percent) in this process as some dehydration occurs—which concentrates the flavor—and all the mold is cut away. A speedier alternative is wet aging, in which the meat is vacuum packed, holding in the moisture. But don't confuse old beef with aged beef, and don't try to age it at home; the process is very specific.

VAQUERO SAUCE

This sauce is great served over steak, chicken breast, fish or almost anything (Pictured at right.)

4 medium tomatoes, cut into 1-inch chunks
1/2 medium onion, coarsely chopped
1/2 pound fresh mushrooms, sliced
1 cup Picante Sauce (page 45)

Cook down tomatoes, then add onions, mushrooms and picante. Simmer over a medium heat until onions are cooked. *Makes 3 cups.*

CHUNKS OF SIRLOIN

This comes straight from our friends at the LX Ranch.

4 pounds lean, boneless sirloin
1/2 cup olive oil
1/2 stick butter, melted
Juice of 1/2 lemon
4–6 tablespoons Worcestershire sauce
1/2 cup chopped fresh parsley
Freshly ground black pepper, lemon pepper and salt, to taste

Have your butcher cut the sirloin steak into "bricks" approximately 3 by 3 by 5 inches. Combine the remaining ingredients and rub into bricks. Let sit at room temperature for 1 hour.

Grill long sides over hot coals for 6 minutes each, and a few minutes on each end. Remove from the grill and let sit for 5 to 10 minutes before carving. With a sharp knife, slice into 1/2-inch slices, and serve immediately. (If there are any leftovers, slice thinly and serve in Chuck Wagon Beef Salad, page 64.) *Serves 8 to 10.*

FAJITA

A real fajita is made with skirt steak, though flank can be substituted.

Marinade:
1 cup oil
1 cup vinegar
1 tablespoon minced garlic
1 teaspoon salt
1 teaspoon cayenne pepper
1 bay leaf

2–2½ pounds skirt steak

Combine all the marinade ingredients. Put the mixture in an airtight container and refrigerate for at least an hour (or overnight, if you have time) to blend flavors.

Trim the excess fat from the steak and place in the marinade for at least 2 hours. Remove steak from marinade and grill over very hot coals for about 3 to 5 minutes per side, occasionally brushing with marinade. Remove from heat and slice into thin strips.

Serve wrapped in warm flour tortillas, with bowls of Pico de Gallo (page 40), Guacamole (page 41), shredded cheese, refried beans, and whatever else you like. *Serves 6.*

FRIED CATFISH

Catfish is one of the few things to be publicly accepted by ranchers and cattleman as an alternative to beef, and it's a beautiful, flaky white meat. Catfish are in most every Texas river, lake and pond, and we all grew up fishing for them. Now they're available farm-raised in any grocery store.

Before we batter our fish, we cut them in half (lengthwise), because if they're too large, the ratio of fish to cornmeal is going to be off. Don't use too much batter for the amount of fish. We use heavy, cast-iron pots, but your favorite deep skillet will do just fine.

6 5–7 ounces catfish fillets

Egg Dip:
¾ cup milk
1 egg, beaten
2 teaspoons seasoning salt
½ teaspoon ground white pepper

Seasoned Cornmeal:
2 cups yellow cornmeal
¼ cup flour
1 teaspoon cayenne pepper
½ teaspoon black pepper
1 teaspoon salt
¼ teaspoon onion powder
¼ teaspoon garlic powder

Vegetable oil, 2 inches deep in skillet

Slice each fillet in half lengthwise. In a shallow bowl, combine the milk, egg, salt and pepper. Combine the cornmeal and spices on a large plate. Dip the catfish fillet in the egg dip, then coat with the seasoned cornmeal. Shake the excess meal from the fish, then slowly place in hot oil (325°) and fry for about 6 minutes, or until the catfish floats. When the fish is ready, the meat will be flaky. *Serves 6.*

101

PICADILLO CARMELA

Picadillo is a marvelous dip for tortilla chips, a great addition to Chile con Queso (page 46), or a tasty filling for a burrito. It's best prepared a day ahead and refrigerated overnight, to allow the flavors to blend.

2 pounds lean ground beef OR venison
   OR other game meat
1 large onion, chopped
2 large cloves garlic, pressed through garlic press
   or finely minced
½ cup sweet pepper, seeded and chopped
½ cup chopped celery
½ cup sliced carrots
½ teaspoon salt
½ teaspoon pepper
2 tablespoons flour
2 cups Beef Stock (page 129)
½ cup skinned potatoes, cut into 1-inch chunks
   (1 large baking potato or 2 small potatoes)
1–2 whole jalapeños (optional)

Lightly brown the meat, onion and garlic in a large skillet over medium-low heat for about 10 minutes, stirring constantly. If meat is very lean, like most venison, first heat 2 tablespoons of oil or bacon drippings in the skillet before adding meat mixture. Add the chopped peppers, celery, carrots, salt and pepper. Add flour to 1 cup beef stock and mix well; add to meat along with remaining stock. Stock should barely cover meat mixture. Lower heat, cover and cook 10 minutes. Add the potatoes (and jalapeños, if you wish) cover and simmer 10 to 15 minutes, until potatoes are tender. *Serves 6 to 8.*

103

PORK RIBS

These are a Texas standard and a real Perini Ranch specialty. We use St. Louis-cut ribs, which are a little larger than a baby back and better trimmed. Ribs are fun because they're something that you really have to eat with your hands. Of course, we always have people who try to eat them with a knife and fork, and you can do it, but why bother? They're perfect for sitting out in the backyard with friends and a couple of cold drinks. Any meat that's this close to the bone is really going to have a lot of flavor; with the rub, I don't think they need barbecue sauce. Try serving a few as an appetizer.

2 racks of St. Louis-cut pork ribs
Rib Rub

Rub both sides of the rack of ribs evenly with the Rib Rub. Place on the pit or in the oven, bone side down, and roast at 250° for about 3 hours. About 15 minutes before the ribs are done, turn the rack over and let the other side get some color. (In the oven, turn the ribs occasionally, then broil to brown.) When the ribs are done, the rack relaxes and droops when you lift it at the center. Cut the ribs parallel to the bones and serve with lots of napkins. *Serves 4 to 6.*

Rib Rub:
2 tablespoons finely ground black pepper
1 tablespoon ground oregano
1 tablespoon paprika
2 teaspoons celery salt
¹/₂ teaspoon cayenne pepper

Combine all the ingredients. Rub over the surface of the ribs to coat.

THE JUDGE'S FRIED CHICKEN

Buffalo Gap became the county seat here in Taylor County back in 1878. When the railroad stopped 15 miles to the north and a town called Abilene sprang up, a rivalry was born. After a year or so there were enough people in Abilene that they wanted to be the new county seat. The decision was made by two judges, one from each town, and the Buffalo Gap judge sided with the opposition. So in retaliation, the people of Buffalo Gap took all the judge's chickens and had a big fried chicken dinner. So every Sunday, in honor of this event, we have the Judge's Fried Chicken at the restaurant.

We cut it up the old-time way—complete with the pulley bone, or wishbone—and we cook it in cast-iron pots. If you're not familiar with cutting a chicken, have your butcher do it.

Vegetable oil, 3 inches in skillet
1 young frying chicken cut into pieces
Flour
Egg Dip (page 101), with salt and pepper added, to taste

Heat oil in a deep, heavy skillet or Dutch oven. Dip the chicken pieces in the egg mixture, then roll in the flour so that each piece is thoroughly coated. Shake off the excess flour and put in hot oil. Fry at 325°, and when the chicken is done it will float to the top. Remember, thighs and legs take a little longer to cook. *Serves 4 to 6.*

105

WILD TURKEY PIE

A great use for your leftover turkey.

1½ cups sliced carrots
1 large onion, chopped
1 pound mushrooms, sliced
2 stalks celery, diced
4 tablespoons butter
¼ cup flour
3 cups turkey broth OR chicken broth (boil the turkey bones)
Salt and pepper, to taste
4 cups cooked turkey meat, cut into bite-sized pieces
4 hard-boiled eggs, peeled and quartered
Piecrust (page 175), omitting the sugar

Sauté the carrots, onion, mushrooms and celery in the butter until onion is clear. Sprinkle the sautéed vegetables with the flour. Stir to combine. Slowly add the broth, stirring constantly, cooking until thickened. Add salt and pepper, to taste, and turkey meat, gently stirring to mix. Add the eggs and pour into a deep 3-quart baking dish.

Roll out the piecrust dough and lay over top. Moisten the edges of the dough and press to the edges of the dish. Prick the crust decoratively in the center. Bake in a 400° oven for 30 minutes until crust is golden. Serve immediately. *Serves 6 to 8.*

BUTTERFLIED, GRILLED LEG OF LAMB

I was raised on lamb and there are plenty of sheep raisers in Texas. This is my version of grilled lamb. We serve it with our Jalapeño Sauce (page 181).

The leg is considered the most flavorful cut of the lamb whether it's roasted whole in the oven or, the way I like to do it, deboned and butterflied into a steak-sized cut you can throw right on the grill.

Marinade (see below)
1 leg of lamb (4–7 pounds), boned and butterflied

Marinade:
6–8 cloves garlic, finely minced or pressed
⅓ cup finely chopped rosemary leaves
   (6–8 sprigs)
1 tablespoon Dijon mustard
1 tablespoon ground black pepper
Juice of 1 lemon
Grated zest of 1 lemon
1 tablespoon salt
2 tablespoons olive oil

Combine the marinade ingredients. Place the lamb in a large zip-lock plastic bag. Add the marinade. Turn and squeeze the plastic bag to be sure all surfaces of the meat come in contact with the marinade. Refrigerate for 2 to 4 hours.

Grill over hot coals, approximately 8 to 10 minutes per side. This will leave it a delicious medium rare. If you must, cook it a few more minutes, but don't overcook!

Serve with Jalapeño Sauce (page 181) or mint jelly. *Serves 8 to 10.*

LX RANCH

Although there has been a Panhandle ranch using the LX brand consistently since its beginning in 1877, there are three definite chapters of its story. It was begun in Potter County in 1877 by two Bostonians on Ranch Creek, a tributary of the Canadian River. W. H. "Deacon" Bates and David T. Beals annually drove herds to Dodge City through about 1884. During the Bostonians' ownership, they were visited occasionally by the cattle-rustling Henry McCarty, a.k.a. Billy the Kid.

In 1884, Bates and Beals sold the ranch, along with 45,000 cattle and 1,000 horses, to the American Pastoral Company of London. Then in 1910, the LX Ranch began its third

phase when it was divided by sale to Joseph T. Sneed Jr., Lee Bivins and Robert Benjamin Masterson. Through additional purchases, the Bivins family acquired the LX brand in 1915 and have used it since. The family of Texas senator Teel Bivins of Amarillo has the use of the LX brand today.

CELEBRATION VENISON WITH GINGER AND WINE

Anytime a cowboy saw a deer or an antelope on a trail drive, he would shoot it and bring it into camp for the cook to serve up. This festive stew is wonderful for a holiday supper, and the lean meat from a leg of venison is well suited to this method of cooking.

4 ounces salt pork, thinly sliced
2½–3 pounds boneless venison
   cut into 1-inch cubes, to yield 4–6 cups
¼ cup flour
1 teaspoon salt
1 teaspoon freshly ground black pepper
2 tablespoons olive oil
1 cup Beef Stock (page 129)
2 cups dry red wine
1 large onion, coarsely chopped
4 large cloves garlic, thinly sliced or minced
2 stalks celery, sliced
2-inch chunk of fresh ginger, peeled and very thinly sliced
1–2 3-inch sprigs fresh rosemary
   OR ½ teaspoon dried rosemary
2–3 sprigs fresh thyme OR ½ teaspoon dried thyme
(1–2 additional cups beef stock and wine, as needed)

Bronc in Cow Camp; *Charles M. Russell; oil on canvas; 1897; courtesy Amon Carter Museum, Fort Worth, Texas.*

In a large Dutch oven, sauté the salt pork slowly, over medium heat, until crisp. Transfer the crisp pieces to a separate dish. Sprinkle the venison cubes with the flour, salt and pepper. Add olive oil to the pan drippings, and quickly brown the venison chunks on all sides, in several batches, 2 cups at a time. Add a little more oil, if needed. Transfer each batch of sautéed meat to a separate container. When all the venison has been browned and removed from the Dutch oven, pour in the beef stock and stir carefully to deglaze the pan and incorporate all the bits that have stuck to the bottom.

Return the venison to the cooking pan, along with the remaining ingredients. Heat just to boiling, then immediately remove from heat. Cover tightly and transfer to a 350° oven. Bake for approximately 2 hours, until venison is tender. Stir occasionally and add additional stock or wine, as needed, to prevent meat from sticking.

Best if prepared ahead of serving time and allowed to cool for 1 to 2 hours at room temperature (or overnight in the refrigerator) and reheated. Serve over steaming hot rice or wild rice with lots of crusty, hot sourdough bread. *Serves 6 to 8.*

109

Cowboy surveying the landscape; *Erwin E. Smith, photographer; courtesy Texas and Southwestern Cattle Raisers Foundation, Fort Worth, Texas, and Amon Carter Museum, Fort Worth, Texas.*

SOUPS, STEWS AND BREADS

SOUPS, STEWS AND BREADS: THICK, RICH AND SON OF A GUN

These are what we call potted dishes, because they were traditionally fixed in big pots or kettles. In that tradition, I think of a stew as something that would go for several days and the more it cooks the better it becomes. Just hang it on the fire and keep adding things, and it's an easy way to feed a lot of people.

A good stew or soup is also a great way to fix a whole meal in just one pot. You can use such a wide range of ingredients, and you don't have to have the premium pieces of meat. You can use brisket and chuck because you're boiling it, which makes the meat more tender. And it's important to have some good marbling in your meat, because that's where the flavor is; if there's no fat to flavor, you're just going to have boiled vegetables. That's why you boil the bone, to get that nice flavor from the marrow.

Left: Trail-Blazin' Beef Stew (page 117).

I'm not recommending this for the average home cook, but there's an old cowboy favorite called Son of a Gun (or sometimes son of

113

BRANDING

The cattle brand is definitely a Texas icon, and it used to be the only way to identify cattle. In the days before fencing, cattle roamed freely between "cow hunts." Unbranded cattle were called "mavericks" and were essentially there for the taking. Needless to say, ranchers often opted for intricate brands that were difficult to alter.

The early Mexican brands were generally abstract designs, with ranchers' offspring using the basic family design with an added curlicue to represent his own herd. The colonists were using brands in the late 1600s, but these Anglicized brands were generally block letters or Arabic numerals. As Texas cattle production headed westward, however, these letters or numerals were often adorned with additional marks that set them apart. It was common to see rockers, bars, circles or slashes on the West Texas ranchers' cattle hides.

By 1848, Texas ranchers recorded their brands with the county clerk, when the law explicitly stated that an unrecorded brand did not constitute evidence of ownership. The brands are still recorded with the county clerk's office in every county where a rancher runs cattle. Brand inspectors, employed by the Texas and Southwestern Cattle Raisers Association, are still on hand at every auction barn in the state, and still use the brands to identify lost or stolen cattle.

something else) stew. This was the first thing made when an animal was killed on the trail. The idea was to use the things that would spoil first: the organ meats. The cook would cut these up, put them in a pot and boil them down to make a thick, very rich soup. They would eat just the Son of a Gun, because it's so rich it didn't take much. These guys were working hard, you know, they weren't going home at night to their air-conditioned house and sleeping in a bed. They were sleeping on the ground and working all day, so they had to eat a lot just to keep going. I've fixed this before, but not to worry—I wouldn't serve it in the steakhouse.

BREADS: FLOUR TO THE PEOPLE

There's a story from a nearby ranch about a cow boss who, whenever he hired a new cowboy, would always ask, "Can you cook?" If the cowboy said yes, he asked him if he could make bread. Because if a cowboy can't make bread, he can't cook.

We Texans like our breads, and I think it's really an important part of the meal. On the chuck wagon, there would always be biscuits or some kind of flat bread with a meal, and it was the carrier for things like beans or gravy. Good bread serves many purposes. When you're out on the trail, you don't have a lot of silverware. So it's useful to have something to sop up some gravy or hold some molasses.

Biscuits or bits of bread were easy to carry, and often on a drive you would have breakfast and then not stop again until dark. So a cowboy might wrap up a couple of biscuits and some bacon in an oilcloth and stick it in his pocket or his saddlebag to snack on later in the day. But as traditional chuckwagon and cook-shack favorites, these breads are at home on fine china, tin plates or paper napkins.

Branding the spring calves; *Bartlett's Art Studio, photography; Clarendon, Texas; courtesy Texas and Southwestern Cattle Raisers Foundation, Fort Worth, Texas.*

115

GREEN CHILE STEW

This is another chuck-wagon variation with a real New Mexican influence. Green chile is really a term for large, mildly hot Anaheim or poblano peppers.

2 pounds lean chuck roast
1½ tablespoons cooking oil
4 medium potatoes, peeled and diced (optional)
½ medium onion, chopped
12 large Anaheims OR poblanos,
   roasted, peeled and cut into pieces
1 teaspoon garlic salt
1 teaspoon salt
6–7 cups water

Cut the meat into ½-inch cubes and brown in oil in a fairly deep pan. Add potatoes, if using, and onions and brown further. Drain off excess fat. Add peppers, garlic salt, salt and water, bring to a boil, and simmer for at least 30 minutes. Ladle into bowls and serve with your favorite noodles, rice or homemade bread. *Serves 6.*

TRAIL-BLAZIN' BEEF STEW

I think of a stew as being chunky and soup as being more liquid, and this is definitely stew—and a real cowboy version. On a chuck wagon you might not have a lot to put in, but at the cookshack you've got potatoes, corn, carrots and all kinds of things to add. You put them in in the order of how long it takes things to cook. When you dip in and get a spoonful, you should get a taste of everything.

6 tablespoons olive oil, divided in half
2 pounds boneless chuck or pot roast, trimmed, and cut into
    1-inch cubes
1 teaspoon garlic powder, divided in half
2 teaspoons ground cumin, divided in half
2 large white onions, cut into 8 pieces each
5 cups Beef Stock (page 129)
3 cups water
4 cloves garlic, minced
9 large red potatoes, cut in half
4 ears corn, cut into fourths
2 carrots, peeled and cut into 1-inch chunks
½ cup coarsely chopped cilantro
1 teaspoon salt
½ teaspoon ground black pepper

117

Heat 3 tablespoons of the oil in a large skillet. Stir-fry meat, garlic powder and cumin. Remove with slotted spoon and put meat in a 6- or an 8-quart stockpot. Add the onions to the skillet with the remaining 3 tablespoons of oil and sauté until soft. Transfer to a stockpot. Add all the remaining ingredients to the stockpot and bring to a boil. Cover, reduce heat and simmer 1½ to 2 hours, stirring occasionally. Add beef stock, as needed. Serve with flour tortillas. *Serves 6 to 8.*

TEXAS CHILI

Of course, chili is a Texas standard. You can season it as hot as you want, and on a cold winter night, you make a big pot of chili and eat it for a couple of days with corn bread or crackers. Again, you don't have to use fancy cuts of meat, and you grind the beef to what we call chili grind, which is a little coarser than regular hamburger meat.

We hosted a chili cook-off for 10 years and, let me tell you, we saw everything in the world—beef, pork, ostrich, you name it. Everybody thinks their chili is the best, and the thing is, in your mind, chili is what your mother served you, even if it came out of a can.

4 pounds chili-ground meat (see above)
1 large onion
2 cloves garlic
1 teaspoon ground oregano
1 teaspoon cumin seed
3 tablespoons chili powder
2 16-ounce cans stewed tomatoes,
    crushed OR 2 pounds fresh ripe tomatoes, diced
2 cups hot water
2 green bell peppers, chopped
3 large red and 3 large yellow sweet peppers, chopped
2–3 jalapeños, to taste
Salt, to taste

Put the chili meat, onion and garlic in a large heavy boiler or skillet. Sear until light colored. Add the oregano, cumin, chili powder, tomatoes and hot water. Bring to a boil, lower heat and simmer about an hour. As fat cooks out, skim off. Add the peppers and salt, to taste, and cook for 15 minutes. *Makes 9 large bowls of chili.*

MEANS RANCH COMPANY

Taking meals in the shade of a chuck wagon is a way of life that stretches back to the 1880s, when Means's great-grandfather John Z. Means came to the Davis Mountains. Cooking was never done inside the house. Up until the 1930s, cowboys and other ranch employees ate at the "chuck shed," a covered area next to the headquarters.

Today the ranch stretches over parts of Culberson and Jeff Davis counties, where, when the chuck wagon is used, roundup and cattle work can last eight to ten days without anyone having to go back to headquarters. Means's favorite chuck-wagon dish, attributed to cook Bill Miller, is called "Delicious." It's a stew

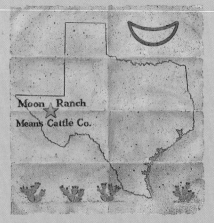

made with leftover breakfast sausage and bacon, along with whatever meat is left from the noon meal, mixed into some kind of macaroni. That, combined with the standard beans, bread and maybe a cobbler completes a typical Means Ranch chuck-wagon offering.

CHUCK-WAGON STEW

This is the standard stew recipe I serve at the chuck wagon, and it's a little heartier than the Trail-Blazin' Beef Stew (page 117). The fat in the brisket and the bacon drippings add flavor to the stew; and this will happen with whatever kind of meat you use. All these ingredients were readily available on the chuck wagon.

8 pounds brisket with excess fat removed
Salt and pepper
Bacon drippings
3 cloves garlic, finely chopped
3 medium white onions, chopped
Water
4–6 medium-sized potatoes
1 cup corn, cut from the cob
28-ounce can chopped tomatoes
1 6-ounce can chopped green chiles

Cube brisket into bite-sized pieces and season with salt and pepper. Brown the meat in bacon drippings and then add chopped garlic and onion. After the meat has browned, add water to cover and bring to a low boil, cooking until tender. When brisket is tender, add the other ingredients—and additional water, if needed—and bring back to a slow boil until stew is fully cooked. I like to leave the pot on the fire for some time to let the flavors marry. Add more seasoning, to taste. *Feeds 20 at the wagon.*

BEEF JERKY SOUP

We think of beef jerky as a snack that comes out of a cellophane package, but it was a way of preserving meat that was used all the time, particularly in Mexico and in the American Southwest. If you don't have a means of refrigeration, you have to do something to keep your meat from spoiling. They would slice meat paper-thin—just shave it—and dry it, and crumble it up in eggs or something, or rehydrate it and make a wonderful beef broth. A cowboy could carry jerky with him and put it in a can with some water, boil it down and add a few seasonings to make beef soup.

8 ounces beef jerky
1 tablespoon cooking oil
1/2 teaspoon ground cumin (comino)
1/2 teaspoon ground black pepper
1 large clove garlic, minced
3/4 cup tomato sauce
1 medium onion, chopped
2 green onions, including about 2 inches fresh green tops, thinly sliced
1 jalapeño, seeded and chopped
1 large ripe tomato, coarsely chopped

121

Soak the jerky in cool water to cover for 2 hours. Drain jerky, reserving liquid. Chop into small pieces. In a large cooking pan, brown jerky in oil. Mix the spices and garlic with tomato sauce and add to the browned jerky. Add the onions, pepper and tomato. Add the soaking liquid and enough water to cover jerky and vegetables. Simmer for 30 to 40 minutes. Serve hot with fresh, warm tortillas. *Serves 6 to 8.*

FIDEO

This is a favorite Mexican pasta stew, and it tends to cook down waiting for the cowboys to come in. The noodles absorb a lot of the broth but the flavors are fantastic. It was traditionally cooked outdoors over an open fire during cold weather as lunch for hungry cowboys, to warm chilled quail hunters or even at home for the children's favorite supper. This recipe comes from the Armstrong Ranch, where it was a family favorite.

¼ cup oil
1 5-ounce package "fideo" pasta OR thin spaghetti pasta
1 large clove garlic, pressed or finely minced
½ cup finely chopped onion
½ cup finely chopped bell pepper
2½ cups boiling Beef Stock (page 129) OR bouillon
½ cup tomato sauce
1 teaspoon ground cumin
1 tablespoon chopped fresh cilantro

Heat the oil in a large Dutch oven. Add the pasta and stir constantly over very low heat until it turns light golden brown (less than 5 minutes). Add garlic, onion and bell pepper and stir constantly about 3 more minutes over low heat. Remove from heat.

Add the boiling stock, tomato sauce, cumin and cilantro. Continue cooking, uncovered, over low heat, stirring once or twice, for about 10 minutes or until liquid is barely absorbed. Fideo should be moist and slippery when served. Serve with Picadillo Carmela (page 103), Ranch Beans (page 155) and fresh, warm tortillas. *Serves 6.*

ANNE'S POSOLE

This traditional Mexican posole is a hominy stew, and it's a standard on ranches in West Texas. This particular recipe is compliments of Anne DeBois, at the Texas Governor's Mansion.

2 cups dried hominy
1 pound pig's feet, cracked
8 cups cold water
1/3 pound ham hock
3 teaspoons Mexican oregano
4 cloves garlic, mashed
2 1/2 teaspoons salt
4 red mild chili pods, stemmed and seeded
2 pounds pork, boned and trimmed
1 teaspoon ground black pepper
2 tablespoons vegetable oil
2 cups chopped onion
1 tablespoon minced garlic
1 teaspoon ground cumin
1 cup water

Rinse hominy and pig's feet in warm water. Place them in a large stockpot with 8 cups of cold tap water and the ham hock and bring to a slow boil. Cook for 15 minutes and skim.

Rub 2 teaspoons of the oregano in palms of hands and crumble into the pot. Add mashed garlic, 2 teaspoons salt and chili pods. Simmer for 2 hours.

Cube pork into 1-inch pieces. Salt and pepper the pork and brown in oil in an iron skillet, a little at a time. After all meat is browned, add the onion and minced garlic. Sauté 3 to 4 minutes over medium-low heat. Add cumin, the remaining oregano and water. Simmer for 10 minutes.

Add the meat mixture to the hominy. Cook, uncovered, 1 1/2 to 2 hours until hominy has burst and the stew is beginning to thicken slightly. Add water or chicken stock, as needed. *Serves 6 to 8.*

123

TOMATO MINCE

Remember, only homegrown, really ripe, fresh tomatoes suit this soup.

4–8 fresh, ripe tomatoes—to yield 4 cups, chopped
2–3 tablespoons finely chopped, sweet onion
2–3 sprigs fresh basil OR cilantro OR parsley
1 tablespoon vinegar
Salt and pepper, to taste
½ cup homemade Texas Mayonnaise (see below)

Chop the tomatoes into chunky dice and combine with the chopped onions. With scissors, cut the basil leaves (or the cilantro or parsley leaves) into thin ribbons and add to the chopped tomatoes.

Add the vinegar and salt and pepper, to taste. Chill. Serve in individual cocktail glasses, cups or bowls, topped with a healthy dollop of mayonnaise. *Serves 6.*

TEXAS MAYONNAISE

1 egg
1 teaspoon Dijon mustard OR ½ teaspoon dry mustard
3 tablespoons fresh lemon juice OR vinegar
Fresh parsley, basil, oregano leaves (optional)
½ teaspoon salt
½ teaspoon ground red pepper
½ cup corn oil
½ cup olive oil

In a blender or food processor, place the egg, mustard, lemon juice, herbs, if desired, salt and pepper. Blend for 1 minute. With blender or processor running, slowly add oils until mayonnaise is thick. Taste and add a little more salt or pepper, if you wish. You may also wish to add more lemon juice, if you prefer a sharper flavor and a thinner consistency. *Makes approximately 1⅓ cups.*

WINTER SQUASH SOUP

This is a delicious use of good Texas squash and a great way to come in from the cold.

3 pounds winter squashes (butternut, delicata, Hubbard or even pumpkin)
1 large unpeeled onion, halved
2 tablespoons oil
¼ cup water
3 cups chicken broth
1 cup milk
1 tablespoon sugar
½ teaspoon ground ginger
½ teaspoon freshly ground nutmeg
½ teaspoon ground red pepper
¼ teaspoon turmeric
½ teaspoon salt

Cut the squash in half and scoop out the seeds. Oil the cut surfaces of squash and onion and place them in a large baking pan cut side down. Bake at 350° until tender and soft, about 1 hour. (Larger squash can take longer.) Remove from the oven and allow to cool until the vegetables can be handled. Scoop out the squash pulp and place in the food processor. Remove the papery outer skin from the onion and add cooked onion to the squash. Purée vegetables until smooth. Add a little broth to make a smooth mixture. Place the puréed squash in a saucepan, add the remaining broth, milk and seasonings. Simmer for a few minutes to allow flavors to blend. Serve with a spoonful of cream, sour cream or crème fraîche. *Serves 8 to 10.*

SEAFOOD GUMBO

This is kind of a catchall dish that has always been really popular down on the Gulf. This recipe comes from my friends at the Hawkins Ranch (page 182). It's fresh seafood but cooked all together with the same idea as a good beef stew, except you don't want to overcook your seafood. Put it in last.

¼ cup flour
¼ cup oil OR bacon drippings
4 medium onions, chopped
2 cloves garlic, minced
2 3-ounce cans tomato paste
4 quarts water
Salt, to taste
3 bay leaves

4 sprigs parsley
1 1-ounce bag pickling spice
1 pound okra, cut (2 packages frozen may be substituted)
4 pounds shrimp, peeled and deveined
4 pounds crabmeat
Tabasco, to taste

Prepare a roux by browning the flour in oil until very brown. Stir continuously, being careful not to let the flour burn. Add the onions and garlic and sauté. Blend in tomato paste while adding 2 quarts of the water (a little at a time). Add the salt, to taste, bay leaves and other seasonings. Simmer 30 minutes. Add two more quarts of water and the okra. Simmer for 2 hours. Add the shrimp and crabmeat, cook for 15 minutes, or until shrimp is done. Remove spice bag and bay leaves. Serve over white rice. *Serves 10 to 12.*

If gumbo is to be frozen, omit the seafood and okra until you reheat the gumbo.

Singing around the chuck wagon campfire *(detail); Charles J. Belden, photographer; courtesy Texas and Southwestern Cattle Raisers Foundation, Fort Worth, Texas.*

127

WHEN STEAKHOUSES WERE STEAKHOUSES

When I was growing up there were a couple of very well-known, old steakhouses about 80 miles from here that we used to drive to all the time. It would take an hour and a half to get there, and we'd have a steak and beer—when we could buy it. Beer was served in big fish bowls that you could barely pick up but they were ice cold. The steaks were so big they would hang over the plate, and they came with lots of French fries and salad. Everyone knew these places: in San Angelo and Lowake. The popularity of the steakhouse waned. I opened the restaurant in 1983. I called it a steakhouse because I wanted

people to know what kind of food we serve. I really believe in not trying to do everything. I think you ought to stick with what you do well. We have chicken, catfish and pork ribs, and people can even get straight vegetable plates, but at least they know what kind of restaurant we are.

GAZPACHO

This cold vegetable soup is wonderful in the summertime, especially if you are fortunate to live where you can get really good fresh vegetables. All of these things grow in Texas. It's obviously not the kind of thing you'd find on a chuck wagon, but it could certainly be made right out of the cook's garden at the cookshack.

1 medium cucumber
4 ripe tomatoes
1 clove garlic, minced
1/3 cup minced onion
1/2 cup minced green bell pepper
1/4 cup olive oil
2 cups tomato juice
1 teaspoon salt
Dash of pepper
1 tablespoon vinegar

Dice the cucumber and tomatoes. Put all the ingredients in a blender and blend for 1 minute. Chill thoroughly before serving, at least 4 hours. *Serves 6 to 8.*

BEEF STOCK

This is so easy to make and so useful, it's a shame to let those bones go to waste. And it's a great broth for soups and stews.

3–4 pounds meaty beef bones
1 large onion, coarsely chopped
2–3 carrots, coarsely chopped
3–4 stalks celery, coarsely chopped
Fresh herbs, to taste: parsley, thyme, rosemary
1 tablespoon salt
1 tablespoon ground black pepper
Water

Far left: Perini Ranch Steakhouse scene.

Roast the bones in a 400° oven for approximately 45 minutes. Place the roasted bones in a large stockpot and add the vegetables and herbs. Add 2 cups of water to the roasting pan, scraping up the browned bits stuck to the pan, and add the broth to the stockpot. Cover the bones and vegetables with salt, pepper and 1 gallon of water. Bring to a boil and skim any foam on the surface. Simmer for about 4 hours, adding water, as needed, to keep the bones covered. Remove from heat and let cool. Remove any fat from the surface, add salt and pepper, to taste, and strain bones and vegetables. Pour into freezer-safe containers and freeze until needed.
Makes 4 quarts.

129

Men dressed for the part act out, for fun, an Indian "pow-wow" for beef. When herds were driven through Indian territory, trail bosses negotiated with local tribes, paying for the right of passage with heads of cattle. The raised right hand is the universal sign for peace. Bonham, Texas; *Erwin E. Smith, photographer; 1927; gelatin dry plate negative; courtesy Texas and Southwestern Cattle Raisers Foundation, Fort Worth, Texas, and Amon Carter Museum, Fort Worth, Texas.*

ONION SOUP

This is our take on the French classic that's great anywhere it's cold out.

3 cups coarsely chopped white onion
2 tablespoons butter
4 cups Beef Stock (page 129)
1½ cups dry white wine
1 teaspoon Worcestershire sauce
1 loaf Sourdough Bread (page 137)
Grated Parmesan cheese

In a large saucepan, cook the onions in butter over low heat about 30 minutes, stirring occasionally. Add the beef stock, wine and Worcestershire sauce. Heat to boiling. Reduce heat, cover and simmer for about 30 minutes. Cut the bread into slices and toast lightly. Place a slice of bread in each soup bowl. Pour hot soup over bread and sprinkle with cheese. Serve immediately. Try this with the Sourdough Bread Chips (page 49). *Serves 4 to 6.*

BEAN BROTH SOUP

Simply delicious!

3 cups broth from Ranch Beans (page 155)
1½ cups Beef Stock (page 129)
Juice of 1 lemon
1 tablespoon bacon drippings (optional)

Heat all the ingredients and simmer for at least 1 hour. Garnish each bowl with freshly chopped white onion. You can also try sour cream, grated cheese or green onion for a garnish. *Serves 4 to 6.*

Humpbacked cattle on the Texas coastal plains; *photographer unknown; courtesy Texas and South-western Cattle Raisers Foundation, Fort Worth, Texas.*

SKILLET CORN BREAD

Corn bread is a traditional Texas bread and there are lots of variations on the recipe and method. Everyone seems to have a personal favorite. People add things like jalapeños, green chiles, fresh corn, a can of creamed corn, grated cheddar cheese and diced onions. I like this recipe because, with the cast iron, you get nice even heat and your corn bread has an even brown crust. Serve it in the skillet and you have a beautiful presentation; the cast iron keeps the corn bread warm.

2 cups buttermilk
2 eggs
1 teaspoon baking soda
2 cups yellow cornmeal
2 tablespoons sugar (optional)
1 teaspoon salt
3–4 tablespoons melted butter
Drop of vanilla

Combine the buttermilk, eggs and baking soda and beat well. In a separate bowl, sift together the cornmeal, sugar, if desired, and salt. Add the buttermilk mixture, butter and vanilla and mix well. Pour into a greased cast-iron skillet. Bake at 450° until golden brown and firm. Let cool slightly and slice like a pie. *Serves 8 to 10.*

WAFFLE CORN BREAD

This is really more of a method because it's basically my corn bread recipe just thinned down a little and poured into a waffle iron. But it's real thin and crispy, and a great form of corn bread. It doesn't fall apart on you and it's got the little holes to hold the butter, beans or molasses.

Thin the corn bread batter, above, with an additional ½ to ¾ cup of buttermilk, milk or water and cook in a well-greased waffle iron. *Serves 8 to 10.*

GRILLED SOURDOUGH
WITH TEXAS ONION BUTTER

This is perfect beside a plate of rare roast beef, potatoes and salad. I practically use it as a utensil with dinner and then for a cold roast beef sandwich the next day.

1 stick butter, softened
¼ cup chopped green onion tops
Minced garlic, to taste
Loaf of sourdough bread

Blend the butter, onions and garlic and refrigerate to set. Slice the sourdough bread approximately ½ inch thick and grill over mesquite fire until grill marks appear. Spread the onion butter on grilled bread. *Serves 6.*

HOE CAKES

These are another contribution of my great-grandmother's and it's just about the simplest form of corn bread there is. Every time my grandmother made these for us she'd always tell stories about her mother. As a child, these things don't really register, but what she was doing was passing on these memories. Now, as I tell these stories to you, my great-grandmother surfaces in the recipes. It's a great way to pass down family tradition.

I think they're great with fried catfish and black-eyed peas, but it's also real chuck-wagon food. All these ingredients would be easy to carry and the hoe cake would have been a nice alternative to a biscuit. Try them with red beans, brisket and fresh sliced onion.

1 cup white cornmeal
½ teaspoon salt
¾ cup boiling water
1–2 tablespoons bacon drippings OR butter

Combine the cornmeal and salt in a bowl. Stirring constantly, add boiling water in a slow thin stream. Beat until batter is smooth.

Pat out hoe cakes with your hand—if batter is too hot, use a spoon. Place on a cast-iron griddle or skillet coated in bacon drippings or butter and fry until golden brown. Turn and repeat. Do not deep fry. *Serves 4.*

HOT, HOT, HOT

We use all kinds of peppers in all kinds of things, from our bacon-wrapped dove breast to the jalapeño cheesecake. Across the board, peppers are packed with flavor, but there's a wide range of intensity when it comes to the heat. Smaller peppers tend to be hotter, in part because of a larger ratio of seeds and veins to total size. Also, remember that there is a big difference between the tangy pickled jalapeños and the fiery fresh ones. No two peppers are quite alike, and they vary in intensity depend-

ing on the stage of the season, so add a little at a time and taste as you go.

For flavor without all the fire, scoop out the seeds and veins before chopping. Wash your hands with soap when you're done, because these juices can really sting some of the more tender areas of the body. If the soap and water don't cut it, pepper lore tells of home remedies from baking soda to milk of magnesia that will neutralize the heat.

SOURDOUGH STARTER

This was a staple on many a chuck wagon and I think it came out of California originally. Every night the cook would feed it a little yeast, some potato and warm water, and the next morning it would have risen. He would mix most of it with flour and make bread, and then, with what was left over, do the same thing that night. But remember the cook's authority: This was the cook's project and if you knew what was good for you, you didn't go near it. People say that, in Texas, you just don't mess with someone's cowboy hat, and the same thing applied to the cook's sourdough starter.

1 quart milk	3 cups flour
2 packages dry yeast	1 medium white potato,
1 cup water	peeled and chopped
2 cups sugar	

Heat the milk to boiling. Dissolve the yeast in water. Pour the yeast-water mixture and milk into a 1-gallon crock (do not use a metal container). Stir in the sugar and flour. Add the potato. Cover and let stand at room temperature 24 hours before using.

SOURDOUGH BREAD

This really makes you appreciate the starter. It's another long process but worth the wait.

1 cup Sourdough Starter (opposite page)
2½ cups water
5 cups flour
3 tablespoons melted shortening
2 tablespoons sugar
1½ teaspoons baking soda
1 tablespoon salt

Mix together the starter, water and flour. Let stand 18 to 24 hours until dough has risen and is bubbly.

Add the shortening, sugar, baking soda and salt to dough mixture. Mix well and turn out onto a floured board. Knead until satiny, adding a little more flour, if dough is too sticky. Knead at least 10 minutes. Divide into 2 or 3 loaves. Place in greased loaf pans. Let rise in a warm place until nearly doubled in size, 2 to 5 hours. Brush loaf tops with a little water, oil or butter. Bake in a 400° oven for 40 to 45 minutes.

For sourdough rolls, pull off golf ball-sized pieces and bake on a baking sheet. *Serves 18 to 20.*

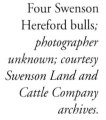

Four Swenson Hereford bulls; photographer unknown; courtesy Swenson Land and Cattle Company archives.

SWEET POTATO PANCAKES

Try these pancakes with thick country bacon, warm honey, cane syrup or with blackberry syrup for a delicious breakfast!

2 eggs, beaten	1 tablespoon baking powder
2 cups milk	1 teaspoon sugar
1½ cups flour	1 teaspoon salt
1½ cups mashed sweet potatoes	½ teaspoon ground cinnamon
1 cup chopped pecans	½ teaspoon ground cloves
½ cup butter, melted	

Mix all the ingredients together, whisking until the batter is smooth. Spoon onto a hot griddle, about 2 tablespoons at a time, for small pancakes—a large serving spoon or half of a ¼ cup scoop makes perfect small pancakes. Cook until bubbles appear and the batter sets. Flip to cook the second side. Transfer to a warm plate and keep warm until a "stack" is ready to serve. *Approximately 48 "silver dollar" pancakes. Serves 8 to 10.*

PAN CAMPO

This is a favorite at the Armstrong Ranch (page 96), in the Wild Horse Desert. This is down near the coast in South Texas and it was the starting point of a lot of the cattle drives. Pan Campo, or "camp bread," is a Mexican bread cooked in a heavy skillet right in the campfire and then sliced like a pie. It's simple, fast and delicious with beans, steak, stew or just gravy.

4 cups flour
2 tablespoons sugar
1 tablespoon salt
1 cup water
6 tablespoons shortening
2 teaspoons baking powder

Mix all the ingredients thoroughly. Roll out on a floured surface to a ¼-inch thickness. Place a round of dough in a skillet. Cook over medium-hot coals for about 5 minutes, until nicely browned on one side. Flip and cook another 5 minutes. Slice into wedges and serve immediately with butter or gravy.

May also be baked on a baking sheet in a 350° oven for about 5 minutes per side. *Serves 8.*

139

Cowboys waiting 'round the wagon; photographer unknown; courtesy Texas and Southwestern Cattle Raisers Foundation, Fort Worth, Texas.

BISCUITS

These were definitely a staple in the early ranch and chuck-wagon days, but we still eat them all the time. In fact, we serve them every Sunday with The Judge's Fried Chicken (page 105). The sourdough biscuits were more common on the wagons. Later, when buttermilk was accessible at the cookshack, with some form of refrigeration and milking cows nearby, buttermilk biscuits were used. There are, of course, other kinds of biscuits like the hardtack, which is a flat, hard, unleavened biscuit. These are both pretty simple to make and are delicious with everything from cream gravy to butter to fresh peach preserves.

BUTTERMILK BISCUITS

141

2 cups flour
2 teaspoons baking powder
½ teaspoon baking soda
¾ teaspoon salt
3 tablespoons vegetable shortening
1 cup buttermilk

Combine the dry ingredients. Add the shortening and mix well with the back of a mixing spoon. Add the buttermilk and mix thoroughly. Roll out dough on a floured board to a ½-inch thickness. Cut into rounds and place on an ungreased baking sheet. Bake at 450° for about 10 minutes, or until browned. *Makes 24 biscuits.*

BAKING POWDER BISCUITS

2 cups flour
3 teaspoons baking powder
½ teaspoon salt
3 tablespoons vegetable shortening
1 cup milk

Combine the dry ingredients. Add the shortening and mix well with the back of a mixing spoon. Add the milk and mix lightly and quickly (do not knead or overmix). Roll out the dough on a floured surface (I use about ⅓ cup flour on a piece of wax paper) to a thickness of ½ inch. Cut the dough into rounds and place on an ungreased baking sheet. Bake at 450° for about 10 minutes. *Makes sixteen 3-inch biscuits or twenty-four 2-inch biscuits.*

MONKEY BREAD

This legendary recipe comes originally from a woman in Albany, Texas, named Anne King, and it's not an easy one. Down here, Anne was famous for her Monkey Bread and used to send it all over the country. Now Anne is gone, but the recipe lives on. It's a unique bread and not something you would have had on the chuck wagon very often; it's more a special occasion kind of bread: maybe Thanksgiving or Christmas.

1 cup scalded milk
½ cup vegetable shortening
1 cup mashed potatoes
1 teaspoon salt
½ cup sugar
1 1-ounce cake of yeast
   OR 1 1½-ounce packet dry yeast
½ cup warm water
3 eggs, beaten
6 cups flour
½ cup butter

Mix together the hot milk and shortening. Add the potatoes, salt and sugar. Set aside to cool to lukewarm. Dissolve the yeast in the water, and add to the potato mixture. Add the beaten eggs. Add 5 cups of the flour, 1 cup at time, mixing well after each addition. Turn out the dough onto a floured board. Sprinkle the dough with ⅓ cup of flour. Knead the dough thoroughly, adding a little more flour if the dough is sticky. Place in a greased bowl, cover and leave to rise for 2 hours.

Melt the butter in a shallow bowl. Roll out the dough on a floured board into a rectangular shape to a thickness of about ½ inch. Cut into 2-inch squares.

Dip the squares into the melted butter and arrange in the bottom of a tube pan. The squares should overlap slightly. Continue to add layers until all the dough is used. Set aside to rise again until double in size, about an hour. Bake at 400° for 25 minutes. Loosen the sides of the monkey bread rings with a table knife. Turn out the monkey bread and let guests pull apart the squares to serve themselves. You may bake in smaller pans, just be sure to reduce cooking time slightly, maybe 15 to 20 minutes. *Makes 1 large loaf.*

143

Rodeo Cowgirl Contestants; *Erwin E. Smith, photographer; ca. 1925–1926; courtesy Texas and Southwestern Cattle Raisers Foundation, Fort Worth, Texas, and Amon Carter Museum, Fort Worth, Texas.*

SIDE DISHES

SIDE DISHES: STAND BY YOUR MAIN

A cowboy might get good and used to the one-pot meals on the trail, but back at the cookshack a side dish can be just as important as the main dish. We are a steakhouse and we're basically built around beef, but as much as we'd like to believe it, man cannot live on beef alone. The dishes that complement a piece of meat are very important here because we get a lot of people who come in and don't get a main course but just get a side dish—a bowl of Jessica's Favorite Green Chile Hominy (page 148) and a salad —and that's great.

The good side stands up to and truly accents the main dish; if it's green beans and new potatoes, that looks good and those flavors really work to-

Left: Green Beans and New Potatoes (page 157).

gether. This part of Texas has a reputation for steaks and potatoes, but Jessica's Favorite Green Chile Hominy and Zucchini Perini (page 150) are wonderful dishes and people just love them.

147

JESSICA'S FAVORITE GREEN CHILE HOMINY

A Perini Ranch Steakhouse signature dish, this recipe was developed with the late Mrs. Louise Matthews, of Albany, Texas, to go with the brisket at her annual party. We visited, considered a whole list of ingredients and, after a little trial and error, Green Chili Hominy was born. It really looks good on a plate; in fact, for large parties we sometimes serve it in cast iron for a more rustic effect. And it's versatile: It's great for breakfast or brunch, a light lunch, or as a side dish with almost any entrée. And it can be prepared ahead of time, frozen, and reheated, and is just as good.

1 cup chopped onion, sautéed
4 15-ounce cans white hominy (drain and reserve)
½ cup hominy liquid
1 tablespoon juice from pickled jalapeños
½ pound cheddar cheese, grated
10 slices bacon, fried crisp and chopped (reserve drippings)
1 cup fresh seeded and chopped poblano
   OR Anaheim peppers
1–2 pickled jalapeños, seeded and chopped (optional)

Sauté the onions in a little of the bacon drippings and put aside. Heat the hominy in a separate sauté pan, stirring often. When heated thoroughly, add the hominy liquid and jalapeño juice, bring back to high temperature and add ¾ of the cheese. When the cheese melts, add half the peppers and bacon and all the onion. Pour into a 9 x 13-inch baking pan and sprinkle with the remaining cheese, bacon and peppers. (At this point it can be refrigerated or even frozen, if you want to make it in advance.) Bake at 325° until cheese on top melts, about 15 minutes (or 40 minutes, if refrigerated). *Serves 10 to 12.*

COWBOY POTATOES

This is probably our most popular side dish with the cowboys
and the ranchers because steak and potatoes are just standard for
this part of the world. It's a real cowboy dish and an easy way to
cook potatoes for 10 hungry people. Besides, you just didn't find
things like sour cream on a chuck wagon. This is easy because
you don't have to peel the potatoes, and the skin adds to the
flavor and the color.

4–5 pounds potatoes, cut into wedges
1 stick butter, melted
1 medium white onion, sliced
1–2 cloves garlic, finely minced
1 teaspoon salt
1 teaspoon ground black pepper
½ teaspoon ground dried oregano

Preheat oven to 350°. Coat the potatoes in butter, toss with
onion and garlic, and sprinkle generously with salt, pepper and
oregano. Place in a baking dish, cover with aluminum foil and
bake for 1 hour, stirring occasionally. After 1 hour, remove the
foil and continue cooking for another 30 minutes to achieve a
nice color. *Serves 8 to 10.*

ZUCCHINI PERINI

I have my cousin Martha Pender to thank for this one. I could get a lot of mileage from a name like Perini—and I do—but this recipe is the real McCoy. Martha is an opera singer from Abilene and picked this up while performing in Italy. I've altered it a bit and I like this because you use fresh vegetables, but with the Italian meat sauce it's also good and hearty. It really is a great way to serve zucchini, which we grow a lot of in Texas. It even works as a main course since it has a little bit of meat in the sauce. For a light lunch, serve it with a salad.

½ pound ground beef
½ pound hot sausage
1 large onion, diced
Dash of salt
Dash of ground black pepper
1 28-ounce can whole tomatoes, mashed and drained
6 ounces tomato paste

¼ cup tomato sauce
2 teaspoons oregano
Dash of garlic powder
2 pounds zucchini, sliced 2 inches thick
¼ cup freshly grated Parmesan cheese

In an oven-safe pan, brown the ground beef, sausage and onion. Add salt and pepper, to taste. Add the whole tomatoes, tomato paste and tomato sauce. Add the oregano and garlic powder and simmer 5 minutes. Add the zucchini. Mix thoroughly, then sprinkle with Parmesan. Bake at 350° until cheese melts and starts to brown, about 10 minutes. *Serves 10.*

FIRE-ROASTED VEGETABLES

This is a technique you can use with just about any vegetable. Grilling vegetables over a live fire awakens the sugars and brings the flavor of the vegetables to the surface, a flavor you don't get in an oven. The color you get by grilling vegetables is spectacular: They look great with a little bit of char around the edges and there's nothing prettier than grilled vegetables with your steak. But be careful not to cook them to mush, they need to have a little firmness.

Wash the vegetables. Use the chart below to determine proportions and cooking times. See that coals are red-hot and about 6 inches below the grill before starting to cook.

Peppers: bell, Anaheim, poblano, 8–10 minutes.
   Cut in half lengthwise and seed.
Peppers: jalapeños, 10 minutes. Leave whole.
Mushrooms, 8–10 minutes. Use whole caps
   with stems removed or trimmed.
Onions: sweet Texas, green and purple,
   10–15 minutes. Slice crosswise into ½-inch slices.
Sweet potatoes, 8–10 minutes. Slice crosswise or
   diagonally into ½-inch slices.
And even eggplant, 10 minutes. Slice crosswise or diagonally
   into ½-inch slices.

Dressing:
½ cup olive oil
2 tablespoons Dijon mustard
2 tablespoons white wine
   vinegar
½ teaspoon salt
¼ teaspoon pepper

Combine the dressing ingredients thoroughly. Toss the vegetables in the dressing. This can be served at room temperature or chilled. Sliced beef may also be added.

152

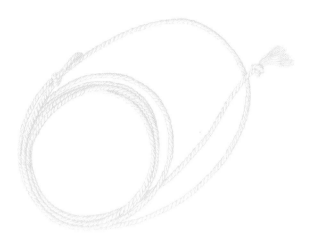

GRILL-ROASTED CORN ON THE COB

I always cook corn this way because I like it with a crunch to it. Boiled corn sometimes reminds me of the corn on the cob I had in grade school that was boiled to death and practically spongy. But this corn is crisp and juicy, and you pick up some of the flavor of the smoke. Choose corn that is young and tender and still in the husks. Cooking corn in the husks is easy and you can peel the husks back and tie them into a handle on the end.

6 ears corn
2 sticks butter
Pinch of ground cayenne pepper
Juice of 1 lime
Salt and pepper, to taste

Remove all but the last 3 or 4 husks from each ear of corn. Place on the grill for about 4 minutes per side, depending on the heat. Turn several times while grilling to expose all sides of the corn to the heat. Corn should be firm with a nice golden, roasted color. The corn silk dries right up and is easy to remove after grilling.

While the corn is cooking, melt the butter in a saucepan and add the cayenne and lime juice. After the corn is cooked, pull back the husks and tie them back with a strip of husk to make a handle. Roll in melted butter and season with salt and pepper, to taste. *Serves 6.*

BAKED RANCH SQUASH

I usually use an acorn squash because they're local and I happen to love them, but you can use anything from butternut to spaghetti squash. You can do this in an oven or on the grill, but either way I like to steam it. The outside is that beautiful green and then you have that orange-yellow inside, and since you put the whole thing on your plate it really makes a nice looking dish. And it comes in its own bowl. If you're not terribly hungry, you might even fix one of these and a salad or some sliced tomatoes and you've got an easy meal.

4 acorn or other winter squash (depending on size)
Salt
Ground black pepper
½ cup (1 stick) melted butter
3 tablespoons brown sugar

Cut the squash in half. Remove seeds and square off the bottoms so that they will sit upright in the pan. Sprinkle with salt and pepper. Brush with butter and sprinkle with brown sugar. Place in a baking dish and add a little water to the bottom of the dish (so that the squash actually steams). Cover with foil and bake at 375° until tender—about an hour. Remove foil, turn oven to broil and brown the tops for 1 to 2 minutes. *Serves 8.*

RANCH BEANS

This is truly one of the basic foods at the chuck wagon, and a staple in this part of Texas. Dried beans were ideal for cattle drives, because you could just throw a bag of them in the wagon and they would keep forever. And they're great today because you can serve them with practically anything. In the summer, we occasionally get them fresh and shell them, but dried are always available. We go through several 50-pound sacks a week at the steakhouse. The key to these beans is the salt pork—known around the cow camp as "streak o' lean, streak o' fat." They make great leftovers as Refried Bean Dip (page 47), and a wonderful Bean Broth Soup (page 131). Beans take longer to cook at higher altitudes.

1 pound dried pinto beans
¼ pound salt pork
3–4 cloves garlic, minced
Salt, to taste
1 tablespoon chili powder

First, rinse the dried beans and remove any stones or dirt. Cut the pork into thin strips and rinse. Cover the beans with water, add the pork and garlic and boil until tender over medium heat (low boil). Beans should always be covered with water. If needed, add more hot water to cover—especially if you want more bean broth. When the beans are tender, season with salt, to taste, and chili powder. Then let the beans sit and absorb these flavors for a while. *Serves 6 to 8.*

Hint: If you want to speed up the cooking process, you can soak the beans in water overnight. Then drain and begin the cooking steps. Also, salting the beans when they first begin to cook can make them tough, so always salt after beans are tender.

SWENSON RANCHES

The patriarch of the Swenson family, Swante Magnus Swenson, is reputed to be the first native-born Swede to set foot on Texas soil. Swenson started out in New York, and in 1850, bought property in Throckmorton, Shackelford, Haskell and Stonewall counties. Swenson's sons Eric and Swen Albin, continued to buy land in King, Motley and Dickens counties. At one time the ranch spanned some 225,000 acres.

The family gave land to establish the city of Stamford, but its lasting contribution to cowboy history is its support of the Texas Cowboy Reunion, an annual competition for ranch cowboys, not professional rodeo cowboys. The Swenson Ranch plays host to

this four-day gathering of riding, roping and roasting. When the cowboys gather to strut their stuff, the chuck wagons circle in equally fierce competition, while ranchers are invited to the Guest Cabin for steak and peach cobbler. The traditional chuck-wagon meal consists of boiled beef, ranch beans, and macaroni and tomatoes.

TOMATOES AND TOAST

Tomatoes were among the first things available canned so were very often used on the chuck wagon. They were also rumored to be good for the stomach and the cook might prescribe them for something like gyp poisoning, a condition brought on by drinking gypsum-tainted water. In fact, this recipe comes from something my father used to make and he did have gyp poisoning. I always use sourdough bread because I like the texture. You can also use fresh tomatoes but you do need to peel them.

1 14-ounce can whole tomatoes
   OR 6 large fresh ripe tomatoes
Butter
Salt, to taste
Pepper, to taste
1 onion, diced
2 Anaheim peppers, chopped
   OR 1 4-ounce can chopped green chiles
6 slices sourdough bread

Cut the tomatoes in half and place in a baking pan. Pat with butter and season with salt and pepper, to taste. Sprinkle the onion and peppers over the tomatoes. Bake at 350° for about 30 minutes. Toast bread on both sides and place on a serving dish. Place half of the tomatoes on toast and reserve the other half and the juice from the baking pan. Mash the remaining tomatoes in juice and cook until juice thickens. Serve over tomatoes on toast. *Serves 6.*

The author, Tom Perini wth Texas lieutenant governor Rick Perry, at the Swenson Ranch Cabin, Texas Cowboy Reunion, Stamford, Texas; *Gerald Ewing, photographer; July 1999.*

GREEN BEANS AND NEW POTATOES

Most people do not season their green beans, but, of course, I use bacon drippings.

1 ½ pounds fresh green beans
  (snap off ends and break beans into bite-sized pieces)
10 whole new red potatoes (small ones are best)
1 tablespoon bacon drippings
¼ teaspoon coarsely ground black pepper
⅔ cup chopped white onion

Put beans and potatoes in a saucepan and cover with water. Add the bacon drippings, pepper and ⅓ cup of the onion. Bring to a slow boil. Cook until beans and potatoes are tender. Add the remaining onion and turn off heat. Let rest for a while and the flavors will intensify. *Serves 6 to 8.*

157

Chuck wagon in cow camp with the fly out for shade; *photographer unknown; courtesy Texas and Southwestern Cattle Raisers Foundation, Fort Worth, Texas.*

BLACK-EYED PEAS

Traditionally, black-eyed peas are considered good luck and I think that's because during General Sherman's March to the Sea, the black-eyed peas were left alone because the Yankees thought they were animal feed. They're often served on New Year's Day to bring luck for the year. We use the snaps (the young pods) to add both a little color and texture. And black-eyed peas are just wonderful with fish; I particularly like to serve them with our fried catfish.

¼ pound salt pork
1 medium onion, chopped
2 pounds fresh, shelled black-eyed peas OR 4 8-ounce
    packages frozen black-eyed peas
1 pound fresh okra OR 1 8-ounce package frozen okra
Salt and pepper, to taste

Slice the pork into ¼-inch-thick slices, then cut slices into ¼-inch-thick strips. In a Dutch oven, cook the salt pork strips slowly in ¼ cup of water, until the water evaporates and the salt pork is crisp and slightly browned. Remove the pork strips from the pan. There will be a salty residue and a small amount of pork drippings left in the pan. Add the chopped onion and sauté until soft. Add the black-eyed peas and enough water to barely cover the peas. Cut the okra into ½-inch rounds, discarding stems, and add to the peas. Bring to a boil, then reduce heat to a simmer. Cook until very tender and season with salt and pepper, to taste. *Serves 6 to 8.*

CARROTS WITH BOURBON SAUCE

Carrots are a wonderful vegetable, but to get cowboys to eat them you've got to put bourbon on them. They're not likely to fall for the old they're-good-for-your-eyes trick; they can already count cattle through 200 yards of brush.

2 pounds carrots, peeled and sliced into 1-inch pieces
¼ cup brown sugar
¼ cup melted butter
2–4 tablespoons bourbon

Steam the carrots to your liking, depending on your preference for crunchy or soft. In a medium saucepan, combine the sugar, butter and bourbon, and simmer over low heat until thick. Pour over steamed carrots. *Serves 6 to 8.*

SQUASH AND HOMINY CASSEROLE

Corn and squash are native to North America and have been in Texas since way before the first herd of cattle wandered up.

3 pounds yellow summer squash OR zucchini
2 large, sweet onions, chopped
½ cup water
1 20-ounce can white hominy, rinsed and drained
2–3 jalapeños, seeded and finely chopped
8–10 ounces longhorn OR Monterey Jack cheese, grated
1 8-ounce package cream cheese, cut into small chunks
1 egg, beaten

Clean and slice the squash into thin rounds. Cook with the onions and water in a large covered sauté pan. Keep over medium heat until just tender, and stir in the hominy, chopped jalapeños, cheeses and egg. Mix well and pour into a 3-quart baking dish. Bake at 350° for about 40 minutes, until bubbling and top is beginning to brown. *Serves 10 to 12.*

161

Cattle tank and windmill; *Bartlett's Art Studio, photography, Clarendon, Texas; courtesy Texas and Southwestern Cattle Raisers Foundation, Fort Worth, Texas.*

MOORE FARMS

When the noon bell rang out in Southeast Texas's Brazos Riverbottom country, Moore family members and hands could count on the kerchief-wearing Kate Thompson to have southern cooking ready to eat. This part of Texas is heavily influenced by the Mississippi Delta—from the accents to the food. Thompson, who cooked for the Moores for more than 40 years, served food straight out of the one-acre garden outside the ranch headquarters.

Alas, when Kate became ill in the early '80s, the tradition of taking meals at the headquarters went by the wayside. Harry Moore, current manager Robert's grandfather, never could find

another cook who suited him. Today, the Moores' operation is strictly a cattle ranch and they use the old headquarters as an office. The family, however, still enjoys Kate's famous "care-mell" pies—Mrs. Robert Moore finally got Kate to tell her how to do it, since Kate never worked from written-down recipes.

BAKED CHEESE GRITS

There has always been a deep southern influence in Texas cooking. Grits is the perfect example. Grits is ground hominy and it's traditionally served for breakfast in the South, but this casserole gives you a great side dish for any meal.

1½ cups water
1 cup dry, quick-cooking grits
1 teaspoon sugar
½ teaspoon salt
1½ cups milk
3 tablespoons butter
1 cup grated longhorn cheese
  OR 1 cup grated Parmesan cheese
2 eggs, well beaten

Bring the water to a boil; add the grits, sugar and salt. Bring back to a boil. Lower heat to medium. Cook for about 5 minutes, stirring constantly, adding the milk a little at a time. Remove from heat. Add the butter, grated cheese and the beaten eggs. Stir thoroughly to combine and pour into a buttered 2-quart baking dish. Bake at 350° for about 30 minutes. *Serves 6.*

The 6666 Ranch chuck wagon in action; photographer unknown; courtesy Texas and Southwestern Cattle Raisers Foundation, Fort Worth, Texas.

CORN PUDDING

Nothing compares to this when it's made with the summer's freshest and sweetest corn.

4 tablespoons butter
2 tablespoons flour
1 cup milk
2 eggs, beaten
2 cups corn, cut from the cob
2 teaspoons sugar
½ teaspoon salt
½ teaspoon pepper

In a large saucepan, over medium heat, melt the butter and stir in the flour. Gradually add the milk, stirring constantly until thickened (3 to 5 minutes). Remove from heat and add the beaten eggs, stirring with a wire whisk. Stir in the corn, sugar, salt and pepper, and pour into a buttered 1½-quart casserole. Place the casserole in a shallow pan half filled with warm water.

Bake at 350° for 45 minutes, or until pudding is set. *Serves 4 to 6.*

163

DESSERTS

DESSERTS: SUGAR AND SPICE

Now you can imagine that cowboys on a long cattle drive didn't have the luxury of dessert very often, but the cooks knew how to do it and they would when the ingredients were on hand. On the trail, dessert was rare; the cook's creativity was always being tested just trying to feed hungry people with what he had. Every now and then he might have come upon some fresh fruit, but it was far from the norm. He did carry a supply of dried fruit—apricots, prunes and raisins mostly—and some form of sugar, most often

Left: Caroline's Fruit Crisp (page 168).

molasses. And every so often the cook probably made some kind of a cookie, and when he pulled out something sweet, that was really a treat.

Today, we still use a lot of the same ingredients, but we just add things that might not have been readily available on the wagon, such as eggs and milk. These desserts have evolved from cowboy classics, some more than others, but they do take advantage of modern conveniences such as refrigeration. And most importantly, they all satisfy that sweet tooth we all seem to develop so easily at the end of a good meal.

CAROLINE'S FRUIT CRISP

This is a favorite of my daughter Caroline, who practically grew up on it. Fruit crisp is a wonderful dessert that works with so many different fruits. We often make it with nice tart Winesap apples, but it's great with any combination of peaches, apples, pears, plums, blackberries or blueberries. (Shown with fresh peaches and nectarines on page 166.)

6–8 large fresh peaches, peeled and sliced—about 4 cups
  (or 4 cups of any other fruit)
Juice of 1 lemon OR of 1 lime (2 tablespoons)
1 tablespoon cinnamon, divided in half
1 stick butter
1 cup flour
1 cup light brown sugar
¾ cup chopped pecans (optional)

Preheat oven to 350°. Place the peaches in the bottom of a 9 x 9-inch baking dish. Sprinkle with the lemon juice and ½ tablespoon of cinnamon. In a mixing bowl, combine the butter, the rest of the cinnamon, flour and brown sugar (and pecans, if using). Crumble on top of the fruit and bake for 30 minutes, or until brown and bubbly.

For a special occasion, top with Peach Brandy Sauce (below), or a little vanilla ice cream or whipping cream. *Serves 6 to 8.*

Peach Brandy Sauce:
4–5 peeled peaches, to yield 1½ cups peach purée
⅓ cup peach brandy

Purée the peaches. Combine with brandy in a saucepan, and simmer 10 minutes over a low heat, stirring constantly.

Tom and Charles
Perini; Reynolds
Bend, Lambshead
Ranch; *ca. 1955;
courtesy Tom Perini.*

169

GRANDMOTHER'S POUND CAKE

This is another Perini holiday tradition; if you look at the
ingredients, you can see why it's called a "pound" cake. The
recipe was my grandmother's, and the cake is great with coffee,
morning or night.

1 pound butter (4 sticks)
1 pound sugar (2¼ cups)
10 egg yolks, beaten until thick and lemon colored
10 egg whites, beaten until stiff
1 pound flour (3½ cups)
½ teaspoon ground mace
2 tablespoons brandy

Preheat oven to 300°. Cream the butter and sugar gradually.
Then add the beaten egg yolks and the beaten egg whites. Add
the flour, mace and brandy and beat vigorously for 5 minutes.
Bake in a deep pan for 1 hour and 15 minutes.

Serve with coffee for dessert or toast it up for breakfast with a
little butter and a tart marmalade. *Serves 6.*

MATTHEWS RANCH

The Matthews and Reynolds families settled in West Central Texas along the Clear Fork of the Brazos River in the late 1850s. The ranch is now home to the descendants of J. A. Matthews and Sallie Reynolds Matthews, who were married there on Christmas Day 1876. Youngest son Watt Matthews restored the early family homesteads including the Stone Ranch, and marked such historic sites as the Butterfield-Overland and McKenzie's Trails.

With Camp Cooper and Fort Griffin nearby, the area was a hub of activity, as described by Sallie Reynolds Matthews in her book, *Interwoven*:

"Beef was bought from the cattlemen, so money was put into circulation where it had been

as scarce as the proverbial "hens' teeth." We were introduced to canned goods, tomatoes, fruits, oysters, milk."

Folks gather daily in the ranch's stone cookshack to share meals with cowboys, family and visitors lucky to be wandering by for Lambshead's famous hospitality.

FLAN

This is a Mexican crème caramel; I will eat this anytime I see it on the menu.

6 eggs, slightly beaten
1 teaspoon vanilla
½ teaspoon salt
2 cups milk
1 cup plus 1 teaspoon sugar
1 tablespoon water
1 tablespoon rum

Preheat oven to 325°. Make the custard by combining the eggs, vanilla, salt, milk and all but ½ cup of the sugar in a food processor and blend until smooth. Then place ½ cup sugar, water and rum in a skillet over medium heat. Stir continuously until syrupy and brown; pour into a greased 7½ x 11-inch, 2-quart baking dish. Add the custard. Place the dish in a hot water bath and bake for 1 hour, or until a knife inserted in the center comes out clean. Allow an additional 30 to 45 minutes baking time if you use a deep-dish flan pan. *Serves 6.*

MEXICAN WEDDING COOKIES

These are deliciously flavored sugar cookies, and you see them all the time at weddings in Texas.

1 cup butter
⅓ cup granulated sugar
1 tablespoon vanilla
1½ teaspoons water
2 cups flour
½ teaspoon salt
½ teaspoon ground cinnamon
½ teaspoon ground cloves
¼ teaspoon ground cardamom (optional)
1 cup chopped pecans
1 cup sifted powdered sugar

Preheat oven to 325°. Cream the butter and granulated sugar until smooth and fluffy. Add the vanilla and water and mix well. Mix the flour with spices and add to butter-sugar mixture, one cup at a time. Add the pecans and blend well. Shape into balls about ¾ inch in diameter (or roll into crescents) and place on a non-stick baking sheet. Flatten the balls slightly with a spoon, if you wish. Bake for about 20 minutes, but do not brown. Cool on the baking sheet for 5 minutes. Roll in the sifted powdered sugar while still slightly warm. *Makes 60 cookies.*

BREAD PUDDING WITH WHISKEY SAUCE

This is another Perini Ranch Steakhouse signature dish and a great way to use leftover bread. Many years ago, Lincoln County, New Mexico, was hosting a Cowboy Symposium and Chuck Wagon Cook-Off, and the grand prize was $3,000. I knew it would take something different to get the judges' attention. We developed this unique recipe, using Texas pecans, sourdough bread, and a whiskey sauce that is really sinful. You've heard of the cook getting into the sauce; well this is the sauce. We won the Cook-Off and have been serving Bread Pudding ever since. I mean, sourdough bread, pecans and a little Jack Daniels—you can't go wrong.

2 eggs
2 tablespoons melted butter
2 tablespoons vanilla
   (Mexican, if available)
2½ cups milk

2 cups sugar
2 cups sourdough bread,
   cut into 1-inch cubes
⅓ cup chopped pecans

Preheat oven to 325°. Beat the eggs, and add the butter, vanilla and milk. Gradually add the sugar and mix thoroughly until sugar is dissolved. Place bread cubes in the bottom of a 9-inch round baking dish. Pour liquid over bread, making sure all the pieces are fully saturated. Sprinkle pecans over bread and push them down into the bread. Bake in the oven for 50 to 60 minutes. *Serves 8 to 10.*

Whiskey Sauce:
½ cup sugar
1 stick butter
½ cup cream
¼ cup Jack Daniels

Childress County, Texas, 1938; Dorothea Lange, photographer; courtesy Amon Carter Museum, Fort Worth, Texas, and The Oakland Museum, Oakland California.

Combine the ingredients in a medium saucepan. Stir constantly over low heat until mixture reaches a low rolling boil. Pour a small amount over the individual servings of bread pudding.

173

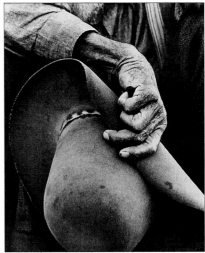

JANE'S SWEET POTATO-PECAN PIE

I have my friend Jane Breed to thank for this recipe, and it is my favorite dessert. It's done in layers and it's a wonderful combination of flavors. Jane's like family and she always fixes this at Christmastime. I've discovered that other family members have developed a taste for it too, so I've got to attack it first if I'm going to get any.

Sweet Potato Filling:
1 cup cooked sweet potato pulp
  (2–3 sweet potatoes, baked)
¼ cup light brown sugar, packed
2 tablespoons sugar
2 tablespoons butter, softened
1 egg, beaten until frothy
1 tablespoon vanilla
¼ teaspoon salt
¼ teaspoon ground cinnamon
¼ teaspoon grated nutmeg
¼ teaspoon ground mace
⅛ teaspoon ground allspice

Combine all the ingredients. Beat until smooth (3 to 4 minutes).
Be careful not to overbeat. Set aside.

Pecan Filling:
¾ cup dark corn syrup
¾ cup sugar
2 tablespoons melted butter
2 eggs
2 teaspoons vanilla
Pinch of salt
⅛ teaspoon ground cinnamon
¾ cup pecan pieces

Combine all the ingredients except the pecans. Mix until opaque (about 1 minute). Stir in the pecans. Set aside.

Piecrust:
4 tablespoons butter, softened
2 tablespoons sugar (optional)
½ teaspoon salt
1 egg
2 tablespoons cold milk
1 cup flour

Cream the butter, sugar, if using, and salt; add the egg and beat 1 minute. Add the milk and beat for another minute. Add the flour and mix just until blended. Shape into a ball, flatten, dust with flour and wrap in plastic wrap. Chill for at least 2 hours.

Roll out the dough on floured board to fit an 8-inch springform pan. Place it in the pan to cover the bottom and sides of pan. Press into place and trim the edges. Chill for 30 minutes before filling.

Fill the dough-lined springform pan with the sweet potato filling. Pour the pecan filling on top—the pecans will rise to the top as the pie bakes. Bake at 325° until a knife inserted into the center comes out clean. *Makes one 8-inch pie.*

COWBOY POETRY

There's not a whole lot to do sitting around the cow camp in the evenings. So it's not surprising that many a cow poke has turned his hand to composing. We're fortunate to have some of Texas's heritage preserved in the words and music of people like Berta Hart Nance, Fran Hedrick and the Gillette brothers. Pipp and Guy Gillette, pictured at right, recording artists, cooks and real cowboys, specialize in rescuing old songs from obscurity—breathing new life into a sometimes forgotten art.

He said, "My chest is hurting mighty
*   bad and I gotta lay me down,*
No need to fetch a doctor, boys,
*   for it's too far to town,*
'Cause I can tell you now
*   this battle I won't win,*
The Head Patron is calling
*   this Old Cocinero in.*
"Go turn my skillets upside down
*   and put my flour away;*
And put those beans back in the sack,
*   they'll not get cooked today.*
"I've cooked you lots of grub, boys,
*   and rolled out lots of dough,*
But I've got to roll my bed now
*   —it's time for me to go.*
I'll not get up and cook for you
*   no more at 4 a.m.,*
The Head Patron is calling
*   this Old Cocinero in."*

— from The Day We Lost
Our Cocinero by Fran Hedrick

DAD'S APPLESAUCE CAKE

This was a favorite of my father's; I remember my mother making it for him all the time. Back then, I always wanted a big sheet cake with lots of frosting for birthdays, but now I love this because it's not too sweet.

1/4 cup butter
1 cup sugar
1 cup cold, unsweetened applesauce
1 teaspoon baking soda
1 cup chopped raisins
1 cup chopped nuts (your favorite)
1 teaspoon ground cinnamon
1/2 teaspoon ground cloves
2 cups flour

Preheat oven to 350°. Cream the butter and sugar gradually. Combine the applesauce and baking soda and then add to the butter-sugar mixture. Add the remaining ingredients and bake in a buttered and floured pan for 40 minutes. *Serves 12.*

TEXAS GINGERBREAD

Gingerbread is a Texas fall and holiday tradition. This one is so moist and delicious it really doesn't need any kind of sauce or topping. Once I start eating it, it goes fast.

2 cups flour
1 pound dark brown sugar
¾ cup melted butter
2 teaspoons ground cinnamon
1 teaspoon baking soda
1 teaspoon grated nutmeg
½ teaspoon ground ginger
2 eggs
1 cup buttermilk

Preheat oven to 350°. Combine the flour and sugar. Cut in the butter. Set aside 1 cup of this mixture for topping. Add the cinnamon, baking soda, nutmeg and ginger to the remaining flour mixture. Stir in the eggs and buttermilk. Do not use an electric mixer. Pour the batter into an ungreased 9 x 13-inch pan. Sprinkle the reserved topping over the batter and bake for 45 minutes, or until done. *Serves 10 to 12.*

Pipp and Guy Gillette singing beside their historic ranch chuck wagon; *courtesy The Gillette Brothers.*

177

STRAWBERRY SHORTCAKE

This is another recipe from my great-grandmother, Mrs. Becky Blake from Abilene. With the Texas biscuits and the warm strawberries, it's just to die for.

2 pounds fresh ripe strawberries
½ cup sugar
8 Buttermilk Biscuits (page 141), sweetened, to taste
1 cup heavy cream

Remove the tops from the strawberries and cut in half. Sprinkle with the sugar and let sit at room temperature until they begin to juice. Put the strawberries and juice in a saucepan and over very low heat, warm thoroughly until the juice begins to thicken. Split the biscuits and scoop strawberries onto biscuit bottoms. Replace top and cover with another spoonful of strawberries. Top with heavy cream. *Serves 8.*

ODESSA'S CHOCOLATE BROWNIES

The best brownies!

2 sticks butter
2 cups sugar
4 eggs
1 cup flour
8 heaping teaspoons unsweetened powdered cocoa
1 teaspoon vanilla
Pinch of salt
1 cup pecans (optional)

Preheat oven to 300° and grease and flour a 9 x 13-inch baking pan. Cream the butter and sugar together and add the eggs, one at a time. Sift the flour and cocoa together. Add to the egg mixture. Add the vanilla, salt and pecans, if desired, and mix. Pour into the greased pan and bake until the top is crispy and firm to the touch, about 20 minutes. *Makes 60 brownies.*

JALAPEÑO CHEESECAKE

This is another favorite dessert at the restaurant and a great combination of flavors. The sweetness and spice really complement the richness of the cheese.

Crust:
2 cups graham cracker crumbs
½ cup pecans
½ cup sugar
1 stick butter, at room temperature

Combine the graham cracker crumbs, pecans and sugar in a food processor and pulse until smooth. Add the butter and mix well until combined. Line the bottom and sides of a springform pan with the crumb mixture.

Filling:
1½ pounds cream cheese
½ cup sugar
1 tablespoon lemon juice
1 teaspoon vanilla
3 eggs
1 jalapeño, seeded and coarsely chopped

Preheat oven to 350°. Combine the cream cheese, sugar, lemon juice and vanilla in a food processor until smooth. Add the eggs and jalapeño and process until well blended.

Pour into the crumb-lined pan. Bake for 1 hour and remove from oven. The top of the cheesecake will have shallow cracks.

Glaze:
1 cup sour cream
1 tablespoon sugar
1 tablespoon lemon juice

Mix together the sour cream, sugar and lemon juice. Spoon the glaze over the top of the cheesecake and bake an additional 15 to 20 minutes. Remove from the oven, cool completely at room temperature and then chill for several hours in the refrigerator. Serve with warm Jalapeño Sauce (below). *Serves 12.*

JALAPEÑO SAUCE

Cowboy Meditating After Noonday Meal in Chuck Tent; Waggoner Estate Ranch, Near Vernon, Texas, 1953*; Bill Carner, photographer; courtesy Amon Carter Museum, Fort Worth, Texas; Copyright Standard Oil Company; Gift of Texas Monthly, Inc. and University of Louisville Photographic Archives.*

6 cups sugar
1½ cups finely chopped green bell pepper
¼ cup finely chopped fresh jalapeño
1½ cups vinegar
1 package fruit pectin (I like Certo)

Bring the sugar, peppers and vinegar to a boil, stirring constantly. Remove from fire and stir in Certo. Pour what you are not going to use within a few days into hot sterilized jars and seal with paraffin. *Makes 4 cups.*

This can also work with cream cheese as a spread or as a substitute for mint jelly on brisket, venison, baked chicken or lamb.

HAWKINS RANCH

When Colonel J. B. Hawkins came to Matagorda County in 1845, his goal was to own a sugar plantation, but when his sugar mill burned down in 1870, he turned his attention to cattle, beginning a ranching legacy that has spanned five generations.

The ranch barbecue house, often uses the traditional "guests' signature" tablecloths. The guests were asked to sign the tablecloth during the party and later, the family would embroider these new names in brightly colored threads.

A typical meal served in this informal house would be barbecued beef or mutton with homemade sauces, along

with rice, black-eyed peas and stewed tomatoes (from the ranch garden), salad, buttermilk biscuits and Odessa's Chocolate Cake (page 185). And the Texas Gulf Coast comes with a lot of seafood. Many meals feature fare from the crab wharf, directly behind the ranch house.

BUTTERMILK PRALINES

Sugar and pecans—it's a natural combination.

2 cups sugar
1 teaspoon baking soda
Pinch of salt
1 cup buttermilk
2 tablespoons butter
1½ cups coarsely chopped pecans
1 teaspoon vanilla

In a large saucepan, combine the sugar, baking soda, salt and buttermilk. Quickly bring to a boil, stirring constantly, until the mixture takes on a creamy texture (about 210° on a candy thermometer). Add the butter and pecans and cook over medium heat, stirring until the thermometer reaches 234° to 238°, or the "soft ball" stage. Remove from the heat and let cool slightly and add the vanilla. Beat with a wooden spoon until the mixture loses its gloss. Drop quickly in mounds on wax paper and let cool. Warning: This can take forever on a rainy day. *Makes 12 to 15 pralines.*

Just in case your batch won't harden, this is delicious as an ice cream topping!

SOPAPILLAS

These sweet tortillas are great for a snack as well as a dessert.

1¾ cups flour
2 teaspoons baking powder
1 tablespoon sugar
1 teaspoon salt
2 tablespoons shortening
⅔ cup milk
2 cups oil
Honey
Cinnamon-sugar

Left: Photographer Bob Moorhouse.

Riding in to the cookshack after a long cowboy day; photographer unknown; courtesy Texas and Southwestern Cattle Raisers Foundation, Fort Worth, Texas.

Combine the flour, baking powder, sugar and salt in a large bowl. Cut in the shortening until mixture is the consistency of cornmeal. Add the milk, mixing just until dough turns into a ball. Turn out onto a lightly floured surface and knead for 1 minute. Cover and let rest for 1 hour. Roll into a 12 x 15-inch rectangle, about ⅛ inch thick. Cut into 3-inch squares. Heat the oil in a large skillet to 375°. One at a time, drop the squares into the oil, turning at once so that they puff evenly. Fry only one at a time so that the oil will remain hot. Brown on both sides and drain on paper towels. Serve hot with butter, honey, and/or cinnamon-sugar to complete any meal. *Makes about 16 to 18 squares.*

183

ODESSA'S CHOCOLATE CAKE WITH WHITE SUGAR ICING

1 stick butter
2 cups brown sugar
2 eggs
4 2-ounce squares unsweetened chocolate
1 teaspoon vanilla
2 cups flour
1 teaspoon baking soda
1 teaspoon baking powder
1 cup buttermilk
Pinch of salt

Cream the butter and brown sugar together. Add the eggs, one at a time. Melt the chocolate in a double boiler and add to the creamed butter. Add the vanilla. In a separate bowl, mix the dry ingredients together and add to the butter mixture. Use a 9 x 11-inch pan, or two 9-inch-round cake pans for a double layer cake.* Bake at 300°, until firm to the touch (about 12 to 15 minutes). Let cool before icing with White Sugar Icing. *Serves 12.*

White Sugar Icing:
2¼ cups granulated sugar
1 cup condensed milk
2 tablespoons butter
1 teaspoon vanilla
Pinch of salt

Place all the ingredients in a saucepan and heat to a rolling boil. Cook for 12 minutes. Remove from heat and let cool. Beat by hand until icing is thick and a spreadable consistency. If too thick, thin down with a little more milk. The icing will harden as firm sugar icing. This is also a great cupcake icing.

For a double layer cake, double this recipe.

CATTLE RAISERS

In Graham, Texas, in 1877, repeated occurrences of cattle rustling led ranchers to band together and form the Stock-Raisers' Association of Northwest Texas. It would eventually grow into the largest rancher organization in the United States, the Texas and Southwestern Cattle Raisers Association. An inspection system, which was created in 1883 and is still in place today, posted inspectors along the trails and at shipping points and terminal markets, and allowed ranchers to reclaim lost or stolen animals. Inspectors used the brands recorded in each county, which are still on record and serve many of the same purposes today. In addition to locating lost or stolen cattle, horses and ranch-related equipment, this organization, which counts members from several states, also represents ranchers in the governmental arena by monitoring state and federal regulations that affect their livelihood. The association moved to Fort Worth in 1893 and is still among the strongest arms of Texas law enforcement.

COUNTRY COBBLER

The fresher and tarter the apples, the better the cobbler.

4 cups cored and sliced tart apples (no need to peel)
2 tablespoons fresh lemon juice
1 cup flour
1 cup sugar
½ teaspoon ground cinnamon
¼ teaspoon grated nutmeg
½ teaspoon salt
2 teaspoons baking powder
1 cup milk
1 stick butter

Toss the apples with lemon juice. In a separate bowl, mix together the flour, sugar, spices and baking powder. Add the milk and mix well. Melt the butter in a 2-quart baking dish. Pour the batter into the baking dish and top with the apples and lemon juice. Bake in a 350° oven for 45 minutes, until the cobbler is puffed and the center is set. Serve warm with a little ice cream or whipping cream. *Serves 6.*

Back at the chuck-wagon camp at the end of the day; photographer unknown; courtesy Texas and Southwestern Cattle Raisers Foundation, Fort Worth, Texas.

BUTTERMILK PIE

This is about as simple a pie as you can make, but boy is it good!

2 cups sugar
¼ cup flour
1 teaspoon vanilla
3 eggs, slightly beaten
1 stick melted butter
¾ cup buttermilk
1 Piecrust (page 175)

Preheat oven to 325°. Mix all the ingredients and beat well. Pour into an unbaked pie shell and bake for about 45 minutes, or until lightly browned and firm. *Serves 8.*

INDEX

Appetizers, 38-55. *See also* Salad
Bacon-Wrapped Dove Breast, 39
Bruschetta with Sourdough Bread
  Chips, Texas, 49
Calf Fries, 38
Chili con Queso (pork sausage
  and cheese), 46
Crab Spread, Hot, 51
Guacamole (avocado), 41
Jalapeño Bites, 48
Nachos, 43
Pecans, Roasted, 54
Picadillo Carmela, 103
Picadillo for Chile Rellenos or
  Holiday Dipping, 55
Picante Sauce, 45
Pickled Shrimp, Texas, 50
Pico De Gallo (salsa), 40
Red Sauce, 53
Refried Bean Dip, 47
Shrimp, Boiled, 52
Shrimp Dip, 44
Shrimp, Grilled, 53
Applesauce Cake, Dad's, 176
Avocado and Grapefruit Salad, 67

Bacon-Wrapped Dove Breast, 39
Baking Powder Biscuits, 142
BBQ Sauce for Beef, 97
Bean(s)
  Black, and Roasted Corn
    Salad, 56
  Broth Soup, 131
  Ranch, 155
  Refried, Dip, 47
Beef, 71-103. *See also* Beef,
  Ground
  about aging, 98; buying and
    storing, 86; internal roasting
    temperature, 90; seasoning, 72
  BBQ Sauce for, 97

Beef Jerky Soup, 121
Brisket, Oven-Roasted, 90
Chicken-Fried Steak (ribeye or
  strip), 96; Cream Gravy for, 97
Fajita (skirt or flank steak), 99
Green Chile Stew, 116
Herb Rub, Texas, 85
Jerky Soup, 121
Laredo Broil (round steak), 89
Pot Roast, Traditional, 93
Prime Rib in the Oven, 89
Ribeye, Ranch-Roasted, 88
Round Steak Rolls, 94
Rub, Perini Ranch Steak, 84
  Ribeye Rub, 89
  Texas Herb, 85
Salad with Hot Bacon Dressing,
  Chuck-Wagon, 64
Salpicon (salad), 63
Sirloin, Chunks of, 98
steak, about bite (tooth) of, 74;
  cooking, 77-79; grilling,
  74-76; hangover temperature, 78
steak, cuts of (filet, flank,
  porterhouse, sirloin, etc), 81
Stew, Chuck-Wagon, 120
Stew, Trail-Blazin', 117
Stock, 129
Tenderloin, 82
Beef, Ground
  Hamburger, 86
  Meatloaf, 95
  Parker Burgers, 87
  Picadillo Carmella, 103
  Picadillo for Chile Rellenos or
    Holiday Dipping, 55
  Texas Chili, 119
  Zucchini Perini, 150
Beer, Buckets of, 37
Beets, Pickled, 66
Beverages, 26-37
  Beer, Buckets of, 37
  Bloody Mary, Cowboy, 28
  Bourbon Milk Punch, 30
  Coffee, Cowboy, 34
  Eggnog, Old-Fashioned, 36
  Hot Chocolate, 35

  Hot Toddy, 31
  Lemon Cooler, Ranch House, 30
  The Martinez (tequila and beer), 29
  Mesquite-A-Rita (margarita), 27
  Perini Martini, 26
  Sangria, Summer, 33; Red, 35
  Tea, Texas, 36
  Tequila Shot, 31
Biscuits, Baking Powder, 142;
  Buttermilk, 141
Black Bean and Roasted
  Corn Salad, 56
Black-Eyed Peas, 159;
  Texas Caviar, 57
Bloody Mary, Cowboy, 28
Bourbon Milk Punch, 30
Bread, 133-43. *See also* Biscuits
  Cornbread, Skillet, 133
  Cornbread, Waffle, 133
  Hoe Cakes, 135
  Monkey, 142—143
  Pan Campo, 139
  Sourdough, 137
  Sourdough, Grilled, with Texas
    Onion Butter, 134
  Sourdough Starter, 136
  Sweet Potato Pancakes, 138
Bread Pudding with Whiskey
  Sauce, 173
Brownies, Chocolate, Odessa's, 179
Bruschetta with Sourdough
  Bread Chips, Texas, 49
Buckets of Beer, 37
Buttermilk
  Biscuits, 141
  Pie, 187
  Pralines, 182

Caesar Salad, Lisa's Favorite, 65
Cake
  Applesauce, Dad's, 176
  Chocolate, with White Sugar
    Icing, Odessa's, 185
  Pound, Grandmother's, 169

Calf Fries, 38
Carrots with Bourbon Sauce, 160
Catfish, Fried, 100
cattle ranching, about, 11-15
Caviar, Texas, 57
Cheese Grits, Baked, 162
Cheesecake, Jalapeño, 180;
    Jalapeño Sauce for, 181
Chicken
    Bacon-Wrapped Dove Breast, 39
    Fried, The Judge's, 105
    -Fried Steak, 96
Chile
    Hominy, Green, Jessica's, 148
    Rellenos, Picadillo for, 55
    Stew, Green, 116
Chili, Texas, 119
Chili con Queso, 46
Chocolate
    Cake with White Sugar Icing, 185
    Hot, 35
chuck box, contents of, 50
Chuck-Wagon Beef Salad with Hot
    Bacon Dressing, 64
Chuck-Wagon Stew, 120
chuck wagons (cook shacks),
    16-17, 25
Chunks of Sirloin, 98
Cobbler, Country, 186
Coffee, Cowboy, 34
Cole Slaw, 61
Cookies, Chocolate Brownies, 179
Cookies, Mexican Wedding, 171
Corn
    on the Cob, Grill-Roasted, 152
    Pudding, 163
    Roasted, and Black Bean Salad, 56
Cornbread
    Hoe Cakes, 135
    Skillet, 133
    Waffle, 133
Cottage Cheese Salad, 59
cowboys, about, 11-15
Crab Spread, Hot, 51
Cream Gravy, 97
Cucumber and Onion Salad, 66

Dessert, 168-87
    Bread Pudding with Whiskey

Sauce, 173
Buttermilk Pie, 187
Buttermilk Pralines, 182
Chocolate Brownies, 179
Chocolate Cake with White Sugar
    Icing, Odessa's, 185
Country Cobbler (apple), 186
Flan (Mexican creme caramel), 170
Fruit Crisp, Caroline's, 168
Gingerbread, Texas, 177
Jalapeño Cheesecake, 180;
    Jalapeño Sauce for, 181
Mexican Wedding Cookies, 171
Pound Cake, Grandmother's, 169
Sopapaillas (sweet tortillas), 183
Strawberry Shortcake, 179
Sweet Potato-Pecan Pie, 174
Dip. *See* Starters
Dove Breast, Bacon-Wrapped, 39
Drinks, 26-37. *See also* Beverages

Eggnog, Old-Fashioned, 36

Fajita (skirt or flank steak), 99
Fideo (pasta stew), 122
Fire-Roasted Vegetables, 151
Flan, 170
Fruit Crisp, Caroline's, 168
Fruit Salad, Autumn, 60

Garlic-Horseradish Cream,
    Roasted, 83
Gazpacho, 128
Gingerbread, Texas, 177
Grapefruit and Avocado Salad, 67
Gravy, Cream, 97
Green Beans and New Potatoes, 157
Green Chile Stew, 116
Grits, Baked Cheese, 162
Guacamole (avocado), 41
Gumbo, Seafood, 127

Hamburger, 86; stuffed, 86
Herb Rub, Texas, 85
Hoe Cakes, 135
Hominy
    Anne's Posole (stew), 123
    Green Chile, Jessica's 148
    and Squash Casserole, 161
Horseradish-Garlic Cream, 83
Horseradish Sauce, Perini, 91

Jalapeño Bites, 48
Jalapeño Cheesecake, 180;
    Sauce, 181
Jerky Soup, Beef, 121

Lamb, Leg of, Butterflied, 107
Laredo Broil (London broil), 89
Lemon Cooler, Ranch House, 30

The Martinez, 29
Martini, Perini, 26
Mayonaise, Texas, 125
Meatloaf, 95
Mesquite-A-Rita, 27
Mexican Wedding Cookies, 171
Milk Punch, Bourbon, 30
Monkey Bread, 142

Nachos, 43

Okra, Pickled, 48
Onion Soup, 130

Pan Campo, 139
Pancakes, Sweet Potatoes, 138
Parker Burgers, 87
Peas, Black-Eyed, 159
Pecan-Sweet Potato Pie, 174
Pecans, Roasted, 54
peppers, varying heat of, 136
Perini Cattle Co., 17-19
Picadillo Carmela, 103
Picadillo for Chile Rellenos, 55
Picante Sauce, 45
Pickled Beets, 66
Pickled Okra, 48
Pickled Shrimp, Texas, 50
Pico De Gallo, 40
Pie, Buttermilk, 187
Piecrust, 175
Pork Ribs, 104; Rub for
    Pork Ribs, 104
Posole, Anne's, 123
Pot Roast, Traditional, 93
Potato(es)
    Cowboy, 149
    New, Green Beans and, 157
    Salad, 58
Pound Cake, Grandmother's, 169
Pralines, Buttermilk, 182
Prime Rib in the Oven, 89

Ranch Salad, Perini, 62
Red Pepper Sauce, Roasted, 94
Red Sauce, 53
Refried Bean Dip, 47
Ribeye, Ranch-Roasted, 88
Ribeye Rub, 88
Round Steak Rolls, 94
rub for meat. See Beef; Pork

Salad, 56-67
    Avocado and Grapefruit, 67
    Beef, with Hot Bacon Dressing,

Chuck-Wagon, 64
Black Bean and Roasted Corn, 56
Caesar, Lisa's Favorite, 65
Cole Slaw, 61
Cottage Cheese, 59
Cucumber and Onion, 66
Fruit, Autumn, 60
Perini Ranch (greens), 62
Pickled Beets, 66
Potato, 58
Salpicon (leftover beef), 63
Texas Caviar, 57
Salad Dressings
    Buttermilk Ranch, 62
    Ceasar, 65
    Hot Bacon, 64
    Poppy Seed, 67
    Texas Mayonaise125
    Viniagrette, 56
Salpicon, 63
Sangria, Summer, 33; Red, 35
Sauce
    BBQ for Beef, 97
    Cream Gravy, 97
    Garlic-Horseradish Cream, 83
    Horseradish, Perini Ranch, 91
    Jalapeño, 181
    Mayonaise, Texas, 125
    Picante, 45
    Pico De Gallo, 40
    Red, 53
    Roasted Red Pepper, 94
    Vaquero, 98
Seafood Gumbo, 127
Shrimp
    Boiled, 52
    Dip, 44
    Grilled, 53; Red Sauce for, 53
    Pickled, Texas, 50
Sirloin, Chunks of, 98
Sopapillas (sweet tortillas), 183
Soup
    Bean Broth, 131
    Beef Jerky, 121
    Beef Stock, 129
    Gazpacho, 128
    Onion, 130
    Squash, Winter, 126
    Tomato Mince, 125
Sourdough. See Bread

Squash
    Baked Ranch, 153
    and Hominy Casserole, 161
    Soup, Winter, 126
Steak. See Beef
Stew
    Beef, Trail-Blazin', 117
    Chuck-Wagon, 120
    Fideo (pasta), 122
    Green Chile, 116
    Posole, Anne's (hominy), 123
    Seafood Gumbo, 127
Stock, Beef, 129
Strawberry Shortcake, 179
Sweet Potato-Pecan Pie, 174

Tea, Texas, 36
Tenderloin, Beef, 82
Tequila Shot, 31
Texas Mayonaise, 125
Tomato Mince (soup), 125
Tomatoes and Toast, 156
Turkey Pie, Wild, 106

Vaquero Sauce, 98
Vegetables, Fire-Roasted, 151
Venison with Ginger and Wine, 108
Venison, Picadillo Carmela, 103
Viniagrette, 56

Waffle Cornbread, 133
Wild Turkey Pie, 106
wines of Texas, 36

Zucchini Perini, 150

ACKNOWLEDGMENTS

I would like to take this opportunity to thank everyone who helped make *Texas Cowboy Cooking* a reality. Thanks to Paschal Fowlkes for the assistance in writing the text, and to Katie Dickie Stavinoha for her research in ranching and Texas history. And a thank you to Rue Judd of Judd Publishing, my agent and producer and editor of this book. Also thanks to the folks at Time-Life Books, particularly Kate Hartson, senior editor, and Jennie Halfant, our project manager.

Thanks to Bob Moorhouse for the spectacular ranch photography, and to food photographer Mark Davis and food stylist Pam Wortham for the exceptional food shots. Also thanks to Gerald Ewing and Lieutenant Governor Rick Perry for the photography at the Stamford Texas Cowboy Reunion.

Thanks for the generous cooperation of the Amon Carter Museum, Fort Worth, Texas; the Museum of Fine Arts, Houston, Texas; the Sid Richardson Collection of Western Art, Fort Worth, Texas; and the Swenson Land and Cattle Company photographic archives for the fine art paintings, drawings, and archival photography included in *Texas Cowboy Cooking*.

There are several organizations that were instrumental in the production of this book. Thanks to my friends at the Texas Beef Council in Austin—the years of friendship and advice have been invaluable. And thanks to the Texas and Southwestern Cattle Raisers Association for their assistance with the cattle ranching history and historic photographs.

Thanks to the Texas ranchers that took time out of their busy schedules to contribute to this book: Boo and Meta Hauser, Hawkins Ranch; Senator Teal Bivens, LX Ranch; Tobin and Anne Armstrong, Armstrong Ranch; the family of Watt Matthews, Lambshead Ranch; Robert and Holly Moore, Moore Farms; Gary Mathis, Ranch Manager, Swenson Land and Cattle Company; Bob Moorhouse, Ranch Manager, Pitchfork Ranch; and Jon and Jackie Means, Means Ranch.

Special thanks to Dale Cronk, head cook of Perini Ranch Steakhouse, and all the Perini Ranch employees that helped to make this book possible.

And, most of all, thanks to Lisa Sanders for all her support, love, and patience. She's heard the stories so many times, she now tells them better than I do.

191

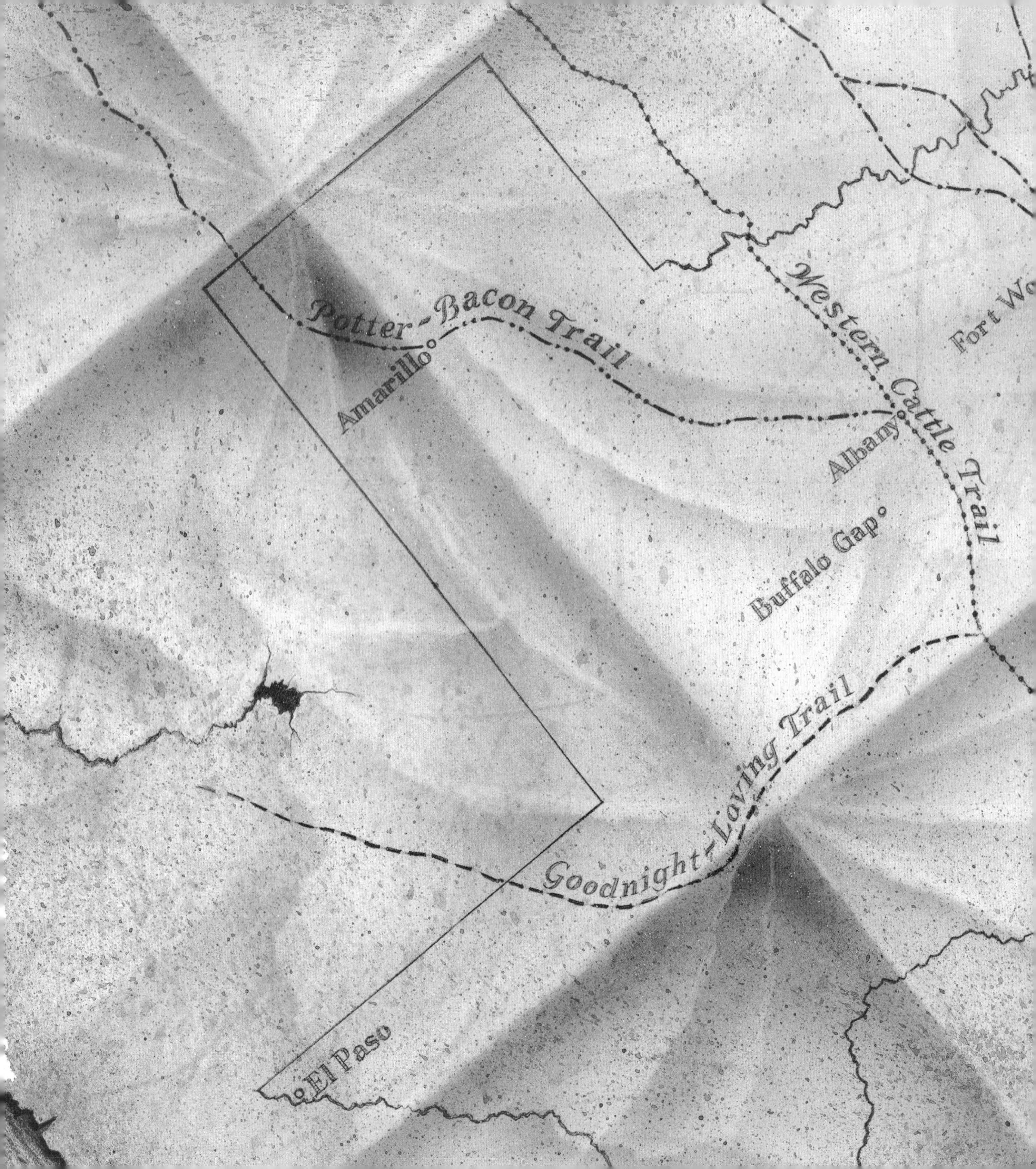
Potter-Bacon Trail
Amarillo
Western Cattle Trail
Fort Wo
Albany
Buffalo Gap
Goodnight-Loving Trail
El Paso